BLOOMSBURY

Concis

Herk

Guide

CW00350609

There are 47 individual Wildlife Trusts covering the whole of the UK and the Isle of Man and Alderney. Together, The Wildlife Trusts are the largest UK voluntary organization dedicated to protecting wildlife and wild places everywhere – at land and sea. They are supported by 800,000 members, 150,000 of whom belong to their junior branch, Wildlife Watch. Every year The Wildlife Trusts work with thousands of schools, and their nature reserves and visitor centres receive millions of visitors.

The Wildlife Trusts work in partnership with hundreds of landowners and businesses in the UK. Building on their existing network of 2,250 nature reserves, The Wildlife Trusts' recovery plan for the UK's wildlife and fragmented habitats, known as A Living Landscape, is being achieved through restoring, recreating and reconnecting large areas of wildlife habitat.

The Wildlife Trusts also have a vision for the UK's seas and sea life – Living Seas, in which wildlife thrives from the depths of the oceans to the coastal shallows. In Living Seas, wildlife and habitats are recovering, the natural environment is adapting well to a changing climate, and people are inspired by marine wildlife and value the sea for the many ways in which it supports our quality of life. As well as protecting wildlife, these projects help to safeguard the ecosystems we depend on for services like clean air and water. All 47 Wildlife Trusts are members of the Royal Society of Wildlife Trusts (Registered charity number 207238). To find your local Wildlife Trust visit wildlifetrusts.org

BLOOMSBURY

Concise
Herb
Guide

BLOOMSBURY
LONDON · NEW DELHI · NEW YORK · SYDNEY

Bloomsbury Natural History
An imprint of Bloomsbury Publishing Plc
50 Bedford Square, London, WC1B 3DP, UK
1385 Broadway, New York, NY 10018, USA

www.bloomsbury.com

BLOOMSBURY and the Diana logo are trademarks of Bloomsbury Publishing
Plc

First published in 2012 by New Holland Publishers (UK) Ltd
This edition published in 2015 by Bloomsbury Publishing Plc
Copyright © 2015 Bloomsbury Publishing Plc

All rights reserved. No part of this publication may be reproduced or
transmitted in any form or by any means, electronic or mechanical, including
photocopying, recording, or any information storage or retrieval system,
without prior permission in writing from the publishers.

A catalogue record for this book is available from the British Library
Library of Congress Cataloguing-in-Publication data has been applied for.
ISBN: PB: 978-1-4729-2235-9
ePub: 978-1-4729-2237-3
ePDF: 978-1-4729-2236-6

2 4 6 8 10 9 7 5 3

Printed and bound in China by Leo Paper Group

Contents

Introduction

This book pictures and describes 180 key commonly used herbs, indicating which parts are used and for what purpose. The information is concise and does not describe gardening or preparation methods, culinary techniques or doses in relation to the healing properties of herbs. Detailed information on all these aspects can be found elsewhere, although a qualified practitioner should always be consulted before using herbs medicinally.

What Are Herbs?

The word 'herb' can be used in several ways. Scientifically, it refers to plants that lack woody tissues, but as an everyday term it also refers to plants used for culinary or medicinal purposes.

Herbs are plants, or parts of plants such as roots, leaves, flowers or fruits, which are used to flavour foods and for their healing properties. Spices are generally regarded as the hard parts of aromatic plants, usually of tropical origin. They include roots, stems, bark, dry fruits and seeds, but some are actually soft parts like flower buds, as in the case of Cloves. The hard parts of many temperate plants also provide herbal products, and can be regarded as spices, Cumin seeds being an example. In the medicinal sense even less distinction is made between herbs and spices, and all medicinal plants tend to be referred to as herbs.

Uses of Herbs

Herbs originally began to be used for culinary purposes for practical reasons – to improve the keeping qualities of meat, and disguise the poor-quality and often rotten food that was all there was to be had. Today, many herbs are used to make food more palatable by adding flavour and easing digestion. They are often regarded as essential ingredients, and are commercially important as preservatives.

Medicinal herbs were once the only remedies available to people, and have long been the mainstay of domestic medicine. Some have been shown to be valueless or even dangerous, but others have proved effective; many have had a long and unbroken history of use.

Therapeutic herbs are used in aromatherapy and other holistic preparations. They are a source of the essential oils used in aromatherapy, as well as to scent pot-pourri mixtures and various cosmetic preparations. They are very concentrated and used in tiny amounts in massages, aromatic baths, inhalations and compresses.

In early herbalism there was no strict division into culinary and medicinal herbs. Many plants can be used for both purposes, and there were others – dye plants, cosmetics, colourants and strewing herbs – that also came within the domain of the herbalist and apothecary.

USING HERBS SAFELY

Herbal treatments are not without risk and should not be used with abandon, and the warnings attached to many of the species in this book should be heeded. Herbs may be harmful if taken in large doses, if toxic parts of a plant are used, if a plant is taken internally, if a person is suffering from a condition that may be adversely affected by using a specific herb, or if an individual is allergic to a particular herb. This book describes the parts of the herb that are usually used and their forms. It does not provide dosages, since these can vary depending on factors such as the condition being treated, and the age and health of an individual. Before attempting *any* treatment other than simple everyday remedies such as tonics, always consult a doctor or other qualified practitioner.

When gathering herbs in the wild, bear in mind that a required herb may have very similar relatives – perhaps harmful or even poisonous – with which it is easily confused. The carrot family, for example, contains many common herbs, but also extremely poisonous plants such as Hemlock. Unless you are very familiar with a herb, always thoroughly check its identity and seek expert advice.

Gathering Herbs in the Wild

The garden is the best place to collect herbs, but if you do choose to look for herbs in the wild there are some fundamental rules that you should follow:

· Damage plants as little as possible, taking only the parts you need, and leaving plants to continue growing.
· Bear in mind that in Britain it is forbidden by law to uproot any plant without express permission of the landowner, and to collect any part, including seeds, of some rare species.
· Do not collect near main roads or in areas where pesticides or other chemicals may have been used.
· If there is any doubt whatsoever about the identity of a plant, leave it alone (see box, page 7).

Growing Herbs

Grown in a garden, herbs can look and smell wonderful, as well as being useful. You can plant them formally, laid out in well-defined patterns, or fit them into borders among other plants. Never spray or apply artificial chemicals to herbs.

Plants from Mediterranean regions, such as Lavender and Rosemary, generally thrive in a sunny position and light, well-drained soil. Woodland species do best in shade, and other herbs, such as Chervil and Valerian, grow happily in partial or dappled shade. In cooler northern areas, tender herbs can be grown in cold frames or moved to grow indoors in winter. Some plants described in this book, such as Cloves, Allspice and Frankincense, are tropical and cannot be grown outdoors in Britain, though smaller species may be grown in a heated conservatory or greenhouse.

Harvesting, Drying and Storing Herbs

If using fresh herbs, pick only the amount needed and use this immediately. Choose young and tender growth. In perennial species pinch off the tips of the main shoots to encourage bushy growth from side shoots. Otherwise pick off lower, older leaves first.

Harvest herbs for later use on a sunny day once the dew has dried out, but before the sun is strong enough to reduce a plant's oil content.

Gather only as much as can be used quickly. Aromatic plants are generally best harvested just before the flowers emerge, while herbs in which the leafy flowering tops are used are best just after the flowers have opened. Pick individual flowers when they are well open and before they begin to fade. Collect seeds as they ripen; it is often easiest to cut off the whole head and handle it by the stalk. Roots are generally best dug up in the autumn, when they are plumpest.

Dry herbs in a dark, warm and airy place, spreading them thinly on open racks or suspending them in bunches. Quick drying is essential to prevent loss of flavour and colour.

Herbs are ready to store when all parts are brittle and break with a snap. Leaves can then be stripped from the stems if required. Seeds are best shaken out of the dry heads. Store dried herbs in airtight containers such as glass jars, opaque boxes or tightly sealed plastic bags, and keep them in a dark place.

Explanations of Some Relevant Terms

ANTISEPTIC Countering infection by preventing the growth of bacteria.

AXIL Angle between leaf and stem.

CALYX Sepals of a flower.

CAPSULE Dry fruit splitting when ripe to release seeds.

DISC FLORET Very small tubular flower with equal lobes, typical of daisies.

DIURETIC Increasing urine production.

ESSENTIAL OIL Volatile oil produced by aromatic plants and providing their characteristic scent and flavour.

LANCEOLATE Shaped like the blade of a spear, widest below the middle.

MUCILAGE Substance that swells and becomes slimy in water.

OPPOSITE LEAVES Pair of leaves at each joint of the stem.

PALMATE LEAVES With lobes or leaflets spreading from a single point.

PERIANTH Sepals and petals of a flower.

PINNATE LEAVES With two parallel rows of lobes or leaflets.

SPUR Projection formed by a flower's sepals or petals.

STAMEN Flower's male organ.

TRIFOLIATE LEAVES With three leaflets.

UMBEL Branched inflorescence, with branches of equal length and all radiating from the same point, typical of the carrot family.

VERMIFUGE Substance used to drive out worms.

Juniper
Juniperus communis

SIZE AND DESCRIPTION Small tree or shrub to 6m tall. Prickly green foliage of female trees is studded with berry-like green cones that ripen to blue-black with a dull bloom in the second or third year.

DISTRIBUTION Native to most areas of the temperate northern hemisphere.

USES Berries are used to flavour marinades, gin, pickles, sauces and game-bird stuffings. They yield an antiseptic and diuretic oil used to treat cystitis. They should not be eaten during pregnancy, and the oil must only be taken internally under medical supervision.

White Willow
Salix alba

SIZE AND DESCRIPTION Silvery-grey tree to 25m tall and with upswept branches. Leaves are narrow and silvery-hairy; they eventually become dull green above. Catkins appear with the leaves; males and females grow on separate trees. **DISTRIBUTION** Found in most of Europe, and western and central Asia. **USES** Fresh and dried bark has long been used for colds and aches, and as a general painkiller. Contains the basis of aspirin, although this is now produced synthetically.

Hop
Humulus lupulus

SIZE AND DESCRIPTION
Perennial climber with
twining stems growing
to 6m tall. Leaves are large,
opposite, bristly and usually
have 3–5 leaflets. Plants are
unisexual, males with branched
clusters of flowers, females with
papery cones.

DISTRIBUTION Native to northern
temperate regions, and often cultivated.

USES Best known for its use in flavouring beer, and grown on a large
commercial scale for the brewing industry. Only the fruiting heads
are used. Young shoots can be steamed and eaten like asparagus.
Hops are said to counter liver and digestive disorders, and used to
make a mild sedative.

Bog-myrtle
Myrica gale

SIZE AND DESCRIPTION
Deciduous shrub
to 1m tall. Leaves
are oval and toothed
at the tips. Red female
and orange male catkins,
borne at the tips of shiny
reddish shoots on separate
plants, appear before the
leaves. Fruits are small
waxy berries. Also called
Sweet Gale.

DISTRIBUTION Locally
common in boggy areas on moors and heaths in western Europe.

USES In Yorkshire, leaves were used for flavouring beer (gale beer)
before hops became popular. Leaves and berries can be dried and
used for flavouring soups and stews.

Common Nettle
Urtica dioica

SIZE AND DESCRIPTION Coarse perennial to 1.5m tall, covered with stinging hairs. Leaves are ovate, pointed and toothed. Flowers are greenish, small and form axillary spikes.

DISTRIBUTION Found throughout northern temperate regions.

USES Aerial parts are rich in vitamins A and C, and iron and other minerals. Young leaves may be added to soups and salads, or made into nettle pudding or beer. Old plants can be toxic and should not be eaten uncooked.

Sandalwood
Santalum album

SIZE AND DESCRIPTION Small evergreen tree to about 10m tall, with slender drooping branches and smooth grey-brown bark. Flowers are bell-shaped, initially dull yellow, turning reddish-purple. Fruits are about 10mm across, and dark red to black. Sandalwood is semi-parasitic on other plants. Also called Indian Sandalwood and Sandalwood Oil Plant.

DISTRIBUTION Possibly native to Indonesia, and cultivated across tropical Asia.

USES Essential oil has a characteristic sensuous aroma and has been extracted from the plant for centuries for use in perfumes, incense and cosmetics. It is soothing and relaxing, and said to help promote restful sleep. Heartwood yields medicinal extracts that are used to treat bronchitis and cystitis.

Common Sorrel
Rumex acetosa

Size and description Perennial to
60cm tall. Leaves are arrowhead-
shaped, with backwards-pointing basal
lobes. Flowers are reddish and small,
with three broad inner segments that
become red and papery in the fruits.
Also called Patriot's Blood and Sour Dock.

Distribution Widespread in northern temperate regions, and
cultivated in gardens.

Uses Salad pot herb from ancient times; tastes metallic if cooked in
an iron pan. Leaves are high in vitamin C, and oxalic acid gives them
a tangy acid taste. They can be added to salads, soups and vegetable
dishes, and sorrel purée is a good complement to fish and egg dishes.

Good-King-Henry
Chenopodium bonus-henricus

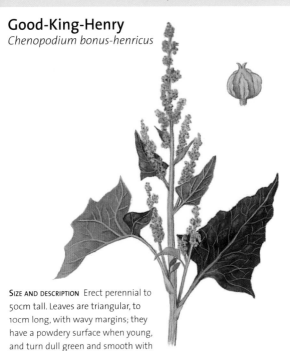

SIZE AND DESCRIPTION Erect perennial to
50cm tall. Leaves are triangular, to
10cm long, with wavy margins; they
have a powdery surface when young,
and turn dull green and smooth with
age. Flowers are very small, greenish and borne on spikes.
DISTRIBUTION Widespread but local throughout Europe, except
the south-east.
USES Young leaves can be eaten raw in salads, older leaves cooked in
stews and soups, and young shoots cooked like asparagus. Seeds have
a laxative effect. Avoid the plant if suffering from a kidney complaint
or rheumatism.

Fat-hen
Chenopodium album

SIZE AND DESCRIPTION Annual to 1.5m tall. Reddish stems are usually covered with a powdery white meal. Leaves are generally oval and pointed, with toothed margins. Flowers are whitish, and grow in small tight clusters on an open spike with leaves at the lower end.

DISTRIBUTION Common across Europe.

USES Young leaves and shoots can be eaten like spinach, or finely chopped and added to stews and soups. They are a good source of vitamin B1, protein, iron and calcium.

Sea Beet
Beta vulgaris maritima

SIZE AND DESCRIPTION Annual, biennial or perennial to 1m tall, usually bushy but sometimes sprawling. Leaves are shiny-green, oval or wedge-shaped, and pointed. Flowers are small, greenish and arranged in clusters on a branched spike. The wild ancestor of cultivated beets.

DISTRIBUTION Grows on the edges of salt marshes and along coastal footpaths in western and southern Europe; rarer further north.

USES Can be used in cooking in the same way as spinach. The tough midribs and large veins should be removed before cooking.

Sea Purslane
Atriplex portulacoides

SIZE AND DESCRIPTION Sprawling, much-branched perennial to 1m tall, covered with silvery meal. Leaves are opposite, oval, thick and fleshy. Flowers are small and arranged in branched short clusters. Also called Lesser Shrubby Orach and Purslane Orach.

DISTRIBUTION Widely distributed in salt marshes and coastal dunes in temperate Eurasia and parts of Africa.

USES Thick, succulent young leaves are edible and can be eaten raw in salads or cooked.

Common Chickweed
Stellaria media

SIZE AND DESCRIPTION Creeping annual to 30cm tall. Much-branched stems bear pairs of pointed oval leaves. Flowers have deeply divided white petals that are slightly shorter than the sepals.

DISTRIBUTION Fast-growing plant native to Europe, but spread by humans and now found in most of the world.

USES Main culinary use is as an addition to salads, or boiled as a vegetable. Leaves contain vitamin C. Also made into an ointment or poultice for inflamed skin, ulcers and chilblains.

Clove Pink
Dianthus caryophyllus

SIZE AND DESCRIPTION Perennial with a woody base, and stems to 50cm tall. Leaves are bluish-green and narrow, and grow in pairs. Petals are rose-pink and frilled at the margins. Flowers are fragrant, with a clove-like spicy scent and flavour.

DISTRIBUTION Native to southern Europe and North Africa, but widely grown elsewhere and one of the earliest herbs cultivated in Britain.

USES Flower petals are used to flavour drinks, syrups, vinegars and salads, or candied for cake decoration. Oil is used in perfumery, the dried flowers in pot-pourri.

Monk's-hood
Aconitum napellus

SIZE AND DESCRIPTION Erect perennial to 1m tall, with paired blackish taproots. Leaves are palmately lobed, with the lobes themselves deeply cut. Flowers are mauve or bluish, with five petal-like sepals, the upper one forming a cowl-like hood. Also called Bear's Foot, Grandmother's Nightcap and Helmet Flower.

DISTRIBUTION Found across much of Europe and northern Asia as far east as the Himalayas.

USES All parts of the plant are poisonous, especially the roots, extracts of which were once used to tip arrows. Used in analgesics to treat pain; a herb that should only ever be prescribed by a qualified medical practitioner.

Opium Poppy
Papaver somniferum

SIZE AND DESCRIPTION
Erect bluish-green
annual to 90cm
tall. Leaves are
pinnately lobed.
Flowers have four
papery white, pink or
purple petals, sometimes
with a dark basal patch.
Large globular capsule has
holes around the rim to release the tiny
seeds. Also called Dream Plant, Fairy's
Charms and Flower of Venus.

DISTRIBUTION Probably of Mediterranean origin; now widespread as
a cultivated and wild plant.

USES Ripe seeds are used in cooking, for sprinkling onto breads and
cakes, and to make a salad oil. Raw opium, obtained from the milky
sap of the unripe capsules, yields various medicinal drugs, including
morphine and codeine. All parts except the ripe seeds, which do not
contain high levels of opiates, should only be used on the advice of
a trained medical professional.

Common Poppy
Papaver rhoeas

SIZE AND DESCRIPTION
Delicate erect,
branching annual
to 70cm tall.
Leaves are
pinnately lobed.
Flowers have four
papery red petals,
each usually with a
dark spot at the base.
Fruit is a globular capsule
with many blue-black seeds. Also
called African Rose, Headache Plant,
Flanders Poppy and Wind Rose.

DISTRIBUTION Common in much of
Europe; rarer in the north.

USES Seeds are used in cakes and
confectionery, sprinkled over pastries, breads and biscuits, and made
into an oil similar in quality to olive oil. Unlike the seeds of Opium
Poppy (opposite), they do not contain narcotic opiates.

Bloodroot
Sanguinaria canadensis

SIZE AND DESCRIPTION Early-flowering woodland perennial to 30cm tall, with blood-red roots. Flowers are white with 8–10 petals, and usually appear before the leaves. Also called Red Puccoon and Snakebite.

DISTRIBUTION Native to eastern and central North America.

USES Poisonous except in mild doses. Fresh root was once used by Native Americans to treat chest and lung ailments. Its only current commercial use is as a constituent of toothpastes and mouthwashes for combating plaque.

Garlic Mustard
Alliaria petiolata

SIZE AND DESCRIPTION Erect biennial to 1.2m tall. Leaves are heart-shaped, toothed at the margins and smell of garlic when bruised. Flowers are white with four petals, and are followed by slender fruits 6–20mm long. Also called Jack-by-the-Hedge.

DISTRIBUTION Found throughout Europe, North Africa, and western and central Asia.

USES Tastes mildly of garlic. Picked before flowering, the leaves can be used in salads and sauces.

Horseradish
Armoracia rusticana

SIZE AND DESCRIPTION Robust perennial to 1.2m tall, with a stout taproot. Large leaves are glossy, stalked, oblong to ovate, and have toothed margins. Flowering stems are leafy, erect and branching. Flowers are white with four petals. Also called Red Cole.

DISTRIBUTION Native to southern Europe and western Asia; cultivated and naturalized in many temperate areas.

USES Grated and mixed with cream, the pungent acrid root yields horseradish sauce. Young leaves can be added to salads. Stimulatory and antibiotic properties; the herb is used for coughs and sinus congestion, and for urinary infections, gout, arthritis and circulatory problems.

Black Mustard
Brassica nigra

SIZE AND DESCRIPTION
Slender annual to
2m tall. Leaves are
pinnately cut and
bristly, with the terminal
lobe much larger than the
other lobes. Flowers are yellow
with four petals. Fruits are slender-
beaked, contain dark brown seeds and are pressed against the stem.
DISTRIBUTION Widespread throughout most temperate regions, and
commonly cultivated.
USES Leaves and flowers can be used in salads, stir-fries and
sandwiches, ground seeds to make a mustard condiment. Warming
stimulant with an antibiotic effect; used to ease muscular pain and
for respiratory tract infections.

White Mustard
Sinapis alba

SIZE AND DESCRIPTION Similar to Black Mustard (page 29), but flowers are slightly larger and fruits have broad beaks and spread out from the stem. Seeds are pale. Also called Salad Mustard and Yellow Mustard.

DISTRIBUTION Occurs across most of Europe and the Near East; introduced into many other areas.

USES Similar to those of Black Mustard. White form is milder. Whole seeds are added to pickles, and seedlings can be used with cress in salads and sandwiches.

Water-cress
Rorippa nasturtium-aquaticum

SIZE AND DESCRIPTION
Perennial to 60cm
tall, with creeping
rooting stems that
grow upwards to
flower. Leaves are glossy, and pinnate
with rounded leaflets. Flowers are white,
small and have four petals. Fruits are
slender, with seeds in two rows on each side.
DISTRIBUTION Grows in shallow water in most
of Europe, North Africa and western Asia.
USES Leaves have a pungent hot taste,
and a high vitamin and mineral content,
particularly of vitamin C and iron. They may
be used in soups and salads, but can be
confused with unrelated poisonous species; additionally, in some
areas wild plants harbour parasitic liver flukes that can damage the
liver. Wild plants are therefore best avoided. Antibacterial and
antifungal properties; used for respiratory tract ailments.

Common Scurvygrass
Cochlearia officinalis

SIZE AND DESCRIPTION Biennial or perennial to 50cm tall. Basal leaves are kidney-shaped, long-stalked and grow in a loose rosette; stem leaves are clasping and fleshy. Flowers are white or occasionally lilac.

DISTRIBUTION Occurs around the coasts of north-west Europe and in the Alps.

USES Relatively bitter leaves may be added to soups, salads and sauces. Fresh leaves were once eaten by sailors on long voyages to prevent scurvy that was caused by vitamin C deficiency. A tonic was also made in the form of scurvygrass ale.

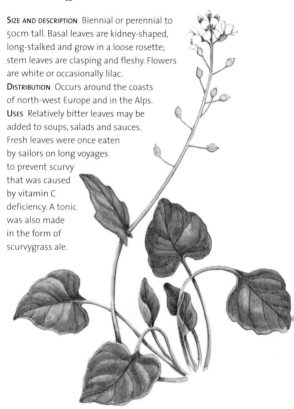

Winter-cress
Barbarea vulgaris

SIZE AND DESCRIPTION
Stout perennial or
biennial to 80cm
tall, with upright
branches. Lower leaves
are pinnately lobed;
upper leaves are smaller
and have wavy margins.
Yellow flowers are borne in
terminal clusters. Also called
Bittercress, Poor Man's Cabbage
and Yellow Rocket.

DISTRIBUTION Common throughout
much of Europe.

USES Hot taste similar to that of Water-
cress (page 31). Once commonly cultivated in Europe as a salad
vegetable. Leaves may be cooked and used like spinach, and young
shoots can be steamed or stir-fried.

Hairy Bitter-cress
Cardamine hirsuta

SIZE AND DESCRIPTION Annual to 30cm tall, with upright stems. Leaves are pinnate with oval leaflets. Flowers are small, white and borne in loose terminal clusters. Fruits are long and narrow pods. Also called Lamb's Cress.
DISTRIBUTION Common throughout Europe.
USES Sharp flavour that is not as hot as that of Water-cress (page 31). May be used in salads or cooked like spinach.

Shepherd's-purse
Capsella bursa-pastoris

Size and description Annual or biennial to 40cm tall. Basal rosette of pinnately divided leaves; stem leaves are stalkless and clasping. Minute white flowers are borne in loose spikes. Fruits are heart-shaped capsules resembling the purses people used to hang from their belts in the Middle Ages, hence the plant's common name.
Distribution Common throughout Europe.
Uses Young leaves, collected before the plant flowers, may be added to salads, soups, sauces and stews, and stir-fried. As a herbal remedy, used mainly for haemorrhages.

Field Penny-cress
Thlaspi arvense

Size and description Annual to 50cm tall. First leaves are oval and pointed, forming a basal rosette; stem leaves are clasping, with arrow-shaped bases and toothed margins. Flowers are small, with white petals, and are arranged in an ascending spike. Fruits are large heart-shaped capsules. Also called Boor's Mustard, French Weed, Stinkweed and Treaclewort.

Distribution Common throughout much of Europe, but less frequent in the north.

Uses Slightly bitter flavour. Small amounts may be finely chopped and added to salads, soups and sauces.

Caper
Capparis spinosa

SIZE AND DESCRIPTION Shrubby perennial with straggly and sometimes spiny branches to 1.5m long. Leaves are fleshy, and circular to ovate. Flowers are white or pinkish-white, four-petalled and have a mass of long purplish stamens in the centre.

DISTRIBUTION Native to parts of the tropics and subtropics, and to cliffs and rocky sites in the Mediterranean.

USES Contains capric acid, and is used as a condiment and in sauces such as sauce tartare. Only the unopened flower buds are eaten, and these must be pickled in wine vinegar in order to bring out the typical flavour.

Cinnamon
Cinnamomum zeylanicum

Size and description Small evergreen tree to 10m tall. Leaves are paired, ovate to elliptical, deeply veined and dark shiny-green. Flowers grow in small, branched yellow clusters, and are followed by dark purple berries. Spice is provided by the fragrant dried inner bark of the young shoots.

Distribution Native to Sri Lanka and the south-west coast of India; cultivated elsewhere in the east and in the West Indies.

Uses Commonly used as a spice in baking, and in drinks like punch. As a remedy, used for coughs, colds and stomach complaints.

Cassia
Cinnamomum aromaticum

SIZE AND DESCRIPTION Closely related to Cinnamon (opposite), though making a larger tree. Spice is obtained from three parts of the tree. Also called Bastard Cinnamon.

DISTRIBUTION Native to China and Burma, and cultivated in many areas of the subtropics.

USES Dried inner bark is very similar to that of Cinnamon and is often used as a substitute for it, though the quills are coarser in both texture and flavour. Dried leaves are used mainly in Indian cooking. Dried unripe fruits are sometimes sold as Chinese cassia buds, and used to flavour sweets and drinks.

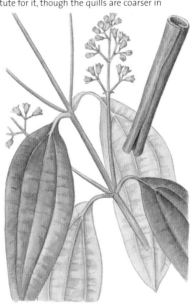

Sweet Bay
Laurus nobilis

SIZE AND DESCRIPTION Bushy evergreen tree to 20m tall. Leaves are wavy-edged and dotted with numerous oil glands; they give off a strong spicy scent when bruised. Flowers are yellowish-green and four-petalled, with males and females on separate trees. Also called Bay Tree, Poet's Laurel, Roman Laurel and Royal Bay.

DISTRIBUTION Native to dry areas of the Mediterranean, and now widely grown elsewhere both as a pot herb and a clipped shrub.

USES Once employed as a strewing herb, and the leafy branches formed the laurel wreaths of ancient Greece. In Roman culture, laurel wreaths were used as a symbol of victory. A culinary flavouring used both dry and fresh since ancient times, in soups, stews and other dishes.

Star-anise
Illicium verum

SIZE AND DESCRIPTION
White-barked
evergreen shrub or
small tree to 5m tall,
with large leaves and
small, many-petalled
yellow flowers. 'Fruit'
consists of eight
single-seeded pods
that radiate from a
central point, forming
a star. Also called
Chinese Anise.

DISTRIBUTION Native to
southern China, where
it is also cultivated, and
to north-east Vietnam.
USES Fruits are harvested
unripe and dried. An
essential ingredient in
Asian cuisines, and used to
flavour dishes such as beef
and fish stews. Oil of anise is used to
flavour drinks. Fruit or seed infusions are used for
sore throats and digestive complaints. Not suitable for young
children, in which it may cause vomiting and seizures.

Ylang-Ylang
Cananga odorata

SIZE AND DESCRIPTION
Evergreen tree to 33m
tall, with smooth ashy
bark. Leaves are large
and wavy-edged.
Flowers are large
and drooping,
greenish at first,
then turning yellow,
with six narrow petals
about 75mm long; they
have a jasmine-like scent.
Also called Macassa Oil.

DISTRIBUTION Native from tropical Asia to Australia, and cultivated
elsewhere in the Far East. Also grown in temperate climates under
conservatory conditions.

USES Flowers yield a heavily scented oil with relaxing anti-
depressant properties, which is used in aromatherapy. Long-term
or excessive use may cause headaches and nausea.

Biting Stonecrop
Sedum acre

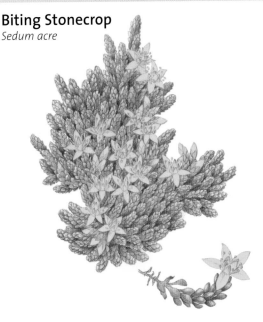

SIZE AND DESCRIPTION Tufted evergreen perennial to 10cm tall. Leaves are fleshy and swollen, crowded on short sterile shoots, and more widely spaced on flowering ones. Star-shaped flowers are bright yellow.

DISTRIBUTION Found across Europe, northern and western Asia, North Africa and North America.

USES Dried and ground leaves have a hot peppery taste and are sometimes recommended as a seasoning, but are slightly poisonous. Once a medicinal herb used for epilepsy and skin diseases, but now used mainly as a corn remover.

Raspberry
Rubus idaeus

Size and description Perennial
with erect, woody biennial stems
to 1.5m tall, armed with weak straight
prickles. Leaves are pinnate, with 5–7 leaflets that are densely white-
hairy beneath. Nodding flowers are white, and borne in small clusters.
Distribution Native to cool regions of Europe, and northern and
central Asia, and widely cultivated.
Uses Yields popular edible fruits, which may be eaten raw and used
in jams, syrups, cordial wines and vinegars. Raspberry-leaf tea is used
for various childhood chills and fevers, and during the later stages of
pregnancy as a muscle toner in preparation for childbirth.

Dog-rose
Rosa canina

SIZE AND DESCRIPTION
Deciduous and often
scrambling shrub to
5m tall, with stout hooked
prickles and pink or white
flowers. Fruits (hips) may be
globose, ovoid or elliptical. Also
called Briar Rose, Cankerberry, Canker Rose and Dog Brier.

DISTRIBUTION Native to Europe, North Africa and parts of Asia, and
naturalized in North America.

USES Hips contain more vitamin C than citrus fruits. If collected after
the first autumn frosts, when they have softened and sweetened,
they can be made into soups, wines, herbal teas, syrups, jams and
jellies. Petals may be used in salads and fragrant jellies, as well as
in perfumes and pot-pourris.

Apothecary's Rose
Rosa gallica var. *officinalis*

SIZE AND DESCRIPTION Spreading deciduous shrub
to 1m tall, with prickles. Flowers are deep pink
and very fragrant. Fruits are bright red and globose.
DISTRIBUTION Native to Europe from Belgium southwards.
USES Both a culinary and medicinal plant, used for flavourings,
perfumes, powders and oils. Hips are used in jams and jellies. Petals
can be crystallized or used to make rose-petal jam. They were once
used for strewing and can be added to pot-pourri. Oil distilled from
the flowers is used in aromatherapy for tension, emotional stress
and insomnia.

Meadowsweet
Filipendula ulmaria

Size and description Perennial to 2m tall.
Leaves are pinnate, with pairs of large
toothed leaflets interspaced with much
smaller ones. Flowers are creamy-white, have a cloying
scent and are crowded into frothy sprays to 25cm long.
Distribution Occurs in most of the temperate northern hemisphere.
Uses Flowers can be used in a syrup for cooling drinks and fruit
salads, leaves to flavour preserves. Contains the chemicals that
produce aspirin, and an infusion from the fresh flowers is employed
for conditions in which aspirin would normally be used.

Agrimony
Agrimonia eupatoria

SIZE AND DESCRIPTION
Perennial with mostly
basal leaves and a long
flower spike to 6ocm
tall. Leaves are pinnate,
with 2–3 pairs of small
leaflets between each
pair of large ones.
Flowers are yellow
and have five petals.
Fruits are crowned
with hooked bristles.
Also called Beggar's Lice
and Church Steeples.
DISTRIBUTION Native
throughout Europe
extending into Asia
Minor and North Africa.
USES Green aerial parts
contain a high proportion
of tannins, which make
the herb useful as a
gargle and digestive
tonic. Long used as a
wound treatment, and
recent research suggests
that it may increase
blood coagulation.

Salad Burnet
Sanguisorba minor

Size and description Perennial with a basal rosette of pinnate leaves and a leafy flowering stem to 50cm tall. Flowers are small and greenish, with four sepals but no petals; they are tightly packed into globose or ovoid flower heads. Also called Pimpernelle.

Distribution Found in dry grassland in most of Europe, parts of the Middle East and North Africa.

Uses Leaves have a mild cucumber flavour. When young, they are good in salads and soups, and as a flavouring for soft cheeses. The plant often remains green during the winter months, and was once much grown at times when fresh salad vegetables were scarce.

Wood Avens
Geum urbanum

SIZE AND DESCRIPTION Perennial to 60cm tall, with pinnate basal leaves and deeply lobed stem leaves. Flowers are bright yellow. Fruiting heads are burr-like, and contain about 70 narrow and hairy fruits, each tipped with a hooked spine. Also called Colewort, Herb Bennet, Indian Chocolate and Star of the Earth.

DISTRIBUTION Native to most of Europe and western Asia.

USES Young leaves can be added to soups and stews. Root contains the same oil as Cloves (page 75) and is similarly antiseptic; it has also been used in place of quinine to counter fevers. Like Agrimony (page 48), contains tannins that act as a digestive tonic.

Parsley-piert
Aphanes arvensis

SIZE AND DESCRIPTION Small annual to 10cm tall. Deeply lobed, parsley-like leaves are divided into three segments, each with up to five lobes at the tip. Tiny flowers are borne in clusters in leafy cups on the stem. Also called Bowel-hive Grass and Fire Grass.

DISTRIBUTION Common in arable fields and on bare ground throughout Europe.

USES Has a mild acidic flavour that makes it useful as an addition to salads. In herbal medicine, used to help kidney and bladder complaints.

Hawthorn
Crataegus monogyna

SIZE AND DESCRIPTION Thorny deciduous tree to 18m tall. Leaves are dark green and deeply lobed. Flowers are white and fruits are dark or bright red. Also called May and Hedgerow Thorn.

DISTRIBUTION Found across Europe and much of Asia.

USES A liqueur can be made from the berries. Buds and young leaves have a light and delicate taste, and can be added to salads. May help to remedy high or low blood pressure, as well as problems associated with the heart such as arterial spasms and angina.

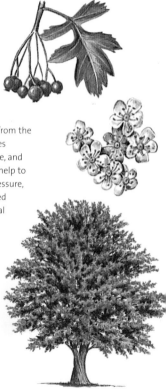

Whitebeam
Sorbus aria

SIZE AND DESCRIPTION
Deciduous tree to 12m tall, sometimes with several trunks; smooth grey bark and an irregularly domed crown. Alternate oval leaves have irregular teeth, and are bright green above and paler green beneath. Flowers are white and grow in branched clusters. Fruits are scarlet. Also called Beam Tree and Chess Apple.

DISTRIBUTION
Native to southern Britain, as well as to central and southern Europe.

USES
Fruits are bitter at first, and best stored until very ripe before use to bring out their sweetness. They may be made into jellies; when dried and ground into a coarse powder they can be added to breakfast cereal, as well as to bread and cake mixes.

Jewel Weed
Impatiens capensis

SIZE AND DESCRIPTION Bushy annual to 1.5m tall, with fleshy and almost transparent stems. Leaves are pale green and waxy beneath. Flowers have five golden-orange, brown-spotted, irregularly shaped petals, and are borne on a slender stalk. Fruits are dry capsules. Also called Orange Balsam.

DISTRIBUTION Native to North America, and naturalized in parts of Europe.

USES Young leaves and stems may be eaten raw in salads or steamed like a vegetable. Green seedpods can be stir-fried or eaten raw. Best known for its skin-healing properties: leaves and juice are used for rashes from poison ivy, nettles and other plants, insect bites and bee stings, and other types of dermatitis.

Broom
Cytisus scoparius

SIZE AND DESCRIPTION Much-branched shrub to 2m tall, with slender whippy twigs that are green and ridged. Small trifoliate or undivided leaves often appear very early. Flowers are yellow, pea-like and numerous. Pods are flattened and oblong, hairy on the margins and black when ripe. Also called Besom, Green Broom and Scots Broom.

DISTRIBUTION Widespread in most of Europe.

USES Pickled flower buds were an Elizabethan culinary item. Contains the alkaloid sparteine, which is used in cardiac treatment and obstetrics, and is a strong diuretic. Should only be used under medical supervision.

Liquorice
Glycyrrhiza glabra

SIZE AND DESCRIPTION Rhizomatous
perennial with erect stems to
1.2m tall. Leaves are
pinnately divided,
the leaflets sticky
beneath. Flowers are
bluish-purple, small,
pea-like and borne
in axiliary spikes.
Also called Spanish
Juice Plant and
Sweetwood, and
Mulaithi in
northern India.

DISTRIBUTION Native
to southern Europe
and western Asia;
also cultivated.

USES A popular
sweet, and used
as a flavouring for
some beers, soft
drinks and various
herbal teas. Roots contain glycyrrhizin, which is approximately 50
times sweeter than sugar. Used as a laxative and for heartburn,
stomach ulcers, colds and coughs, as well as to mask the flavour
of unpleasant-tasting medicines.

Fenugreek
Trigonella foenum-graecum

SIZE AND DESCRIPTION Annual to 50cm tall, with trifoliate leaves that have toothed leaflets. Pea-like flowers are yellow-white and tinged violet at the bases. Pods are to 14cm long, narrow and slightly curved, with as many as 20 very hard, yellow-brown seeds. Also called Greek Clover and Greek Hay.

DISTRIBUTION Probably native to south-west Asia, and widely naturalized and cultivated in southern and central Europe and elsewhere.

USES One of the oldest cultivated plants in the world, recorded in Mesopotamia (present-day Iraq) as far back as 4000BC. Seeds are often added to curries and preserves; when grown like cress, they impart a mild curry flavour to salads. Rich in vitamins and minerals, particularly calcium, and thought to be good for the digestion.

Alexandrian Senna
Senna alexandrina

Size and description
Small shrub about
50cm tall. Leaves are
pinnate with all the
lanceolate leaflets in pairs.
Flowers are yellow, five-
petalled and borne in erect
loose spikes. Pods are about
2.5cm wide and flattened.
Also called True Senna.

Distribution
Native to semi-
desert regions of Somalia and
Yemen, and cultivated in Asia.

Uses
Sennas are probably the
best-known laxatives; the active chemicals, called anthroquinone
glycosides, are found in the leaves and, particularly, the pods. Usually
mixed in a syrup with other herbs and spices such as Cinnamon,
Ginger or Liquorice to make it more palatable.

Tamarind
Tamarindus indica

SIZE AND DESCRIPTION

Densely foliaged
evergreen tree to
30m tall. Leaves are
pinnately divided
into 10–20 pairs of
closely set leaflets.
Flowers are small,
creamy yellow and
red-veined. Pods
are pendulous and
brown, to 2cm
long, and contain
seeds embedded in
a yellow pulp. Also
called Indian Date.

DISTRIBUTION

Possibly native to
tropical Africa,
although it is
unknown in the
wild. Widely cultivated
in India and other tropical parts of the world.

USES Usually sold as a paste or a block that is soaked in hot water
and sieved before use. Sharp rich flavour makes it useful as a culinary
aid in curries, chutneys, sauces and drinks. Used locally for fevers
brought on by the hot winds. Rich in glucosides, and citric, tartric
and malic acids.

Nasturtium
Tropaeolum majus

SIZE AND DESCRIPTION Sprawling or climbing annual with stems to 2m long. Leaves are parasol-shaped; stalk is attached to the centre of the blade. Flowers are orange, yellow or red, to 60mm across and with a backwards-pointing spur. Fruits are three-lobed.

DISTRIBUTION Native to Peru, and widely cultivated in a variety of other colour forms.

USES Peppery-tasting flowers can be added to salads, the flowers and leaves used for tea, and the young pickled fruits used instead of the buds of Caper (page 37). All parts are rich in vitamin C and antibiotic sulphur compounds that may combat infection. More than 15g at a time should not be eaten.

Rose-scented Geranium
Pelargonium graveolens

SIZE AND DESCRIPTION
Perennial to 2m tall, with fragrant, palmately lobed leaves. Flowers are pink or mauve, and are carried in loose umbels. Also called Rose Geranium.

DISTRIBUTION Native to South Africa, and grown in most parts of the world.

USES Intoduced to England in the mid-17th century, and frequently used by the Victorians as houseplants to scent the home. One of the ornamental garden geraniums, which yield fragrances such as rose, lemon and mint. This species has rose-scented foliage, and the fresh or dried leaves may be used to flavour custards, ice creams, jellies, cakes and dessert sauces. Essential oil from the plant is used in perfumery, cosmetics and aromatherapy. Also used in food flavourings, and in fragrant items for the home such as pot-pourri and scented candles.

Castor Oil Plant
Ricinus communis

SIZE AND DESCRIPTION
Robust suckering
perennial to 12m
tall. Leaves are
palmate, glossy
and to 45cm across
with 5–9 lobes.
Spikes are stout,
with greenish male
flowers below
prickly-looking
reddish clusters of female flowers. Fruits are greenish to reddish-
purple, to 2cm long, globular and spiky. Also called Jonah's Gourd,
Mole Bean, Palms of Christ and Steadfast.

DISTRIBUTION Native to the tropics, and widely grown and naturalized
in many areas.

USES Castor oil is obtained from the crushed seeds, and is used in
engine fuels, lubricants, paints, varnishes and insect repellents. It is
also a mild laxative. Seeds contain the poison ricin and are very toxic.

Rue
Ruta graveolens

SIZE AND DESCRIPTION
Aromatic evergreen shrub
to 45cm tall. Leaves are grey-
green and pinnately divided.
Flowers have four yellow petals,
each with an incurved hooded tip.
Also called Bitter Herb, Herb of Grace and Serving Man's Joy.

DISTRIBUTION Native to the eastern Mediterranean, and widely grown
and sometimes naturalized elsewhere.

USES Aerial parts yield an oil that is used in small doses to strengthen
blood vessels and treat colic. Sometimes taken as a bitter tea to expel
worms. Sap can cause a strong allergic reaction on contact with the
skin. Toxic in large doses and should only be used under medical
supervision, and never during pregnancy.

Frankincense
Boswellia sacra

SIZE AND DESCRIPTION
Evergreen shrub or small, papery-barked tree to 6m tall. Leaves are pinnate, with spike-like clusters of small, waxy white flowers in their axils.

DISTRIBUTION Native to Somalia and Arabia. Recent studies have indicated that the trees are declining because of over-exploitation.

USES A major ingredient of sacred incense, known to have been employed since ancient times by cultures including the Egyptians, Babylonians and ancient Greeks. Frankincense is extracted from the gum-like resin of several closely related species, of which this is one of the most important. When employed in aromatherapy, the oil is usually blended with other oils, and used for wounds, scars, and bacterial and fungal infections. Frankincense oil is also used as an ingredient in soaps, cosmetics and perfumes.

Surinam Quassia-wood
Quassia amara

SIZE AND DESCRIPTION
Shrub or small tree
to 3m tall (rarely
to 8m). Leaves are
pinnate, and divided
into five leaflets.
Flowers are bright
red on the outside
and white inside,
tubular and borne
in clusters at the
ends of the twigs.
Also called Bitter
Ash and Bitter Wood.

DISTRIBUTION Native to tropical
America, and also widely planted
outside its native range.

USES Both the bark and roots
contain bitter principles that were
once used to treat dysentery, and
are the source of the mixer drink
bitters. In herbal medicine, used
for digestive disorders, fevers and
intestinal worms, and can be applied topically as an insect repellent.
Surinam Quassia-wood should not be confused with the green-
flowered tree from the West Indies, Quassia-wood (*Picrasma excelsa*),
from which wood chips boiled in water provide an insecticide.

Cascara Sagrada
Rhamnus purshiana

SIZE AND DESCRIPTION
Small deciduous
shrub or tree to
12m tall, with pale
greyish bark. Leaves
are prominently
veined, and there
are clusters of tiny
greenish flowers in
the axils. Berries are
initially bright red,
turning purplish-
black when ripe. Also
called Californian
Bearberry.

DISTRIBUTION Native
to North America.

USES Dried, aged
bark was used for
centuries by Native
Americans as a
laxative. Combined
with pleasantly aromatic herbs, it is used for frail or convalescent
people, and by vets for treating dogs. It is exported to Europe, where
it has replaced remedies derived from local species. Athough used by
immigrant Americans since the late 19th century, it is now banned in
over-the-counter medicines due to its detrimental association with
side effects on the digestion and potentially carcinogenic effects. It
should only be used under medical supervision.

Lime
Tilia x vulgaris

Size and description Tall and narrow-crowned deciduous tree to 46m tall. Leaves are broad, heart-shaped and often sticky with sap. Flowers are yellowish-white, fragrant and hang in a cluster beneath an oblong wing-like bract.

Distribution Naturally occurring hybrid between two European species; widely planted as a street tree.

Uses Tea made from the fragrant flowers may be used for nervous disorders, migraines and insomnia. Flowers may also be beneficial for certain circulatory disorders, and for colds and bronchial complaints.

Marsh-mallow
Althaea officinalis

SIZE AND DESCRIPTION Densely grey-hairy perennial to 2m tall. Leaves are large-toothed and sometimes palmately lobed. Flowers are lilac-pink with shallowly notched petals, and grow on tall spikes.

DISTRIBUTION Native to Europe, North Africa and western Asia.

USES A sweet is made from the roots. Young leaves and flowers may be used in salads. Plant has a high mucilage content, and is used to reduce inflammation of the stomach, make a gargle for throat and mouth infections, and relieve pain from cystitis.

Common Mallow
Malva sylvestris

SIZE AND DESCRIPTION Perennial to 1.5m tall, with a thick and hairy stem that may be erect or spreading. Leaves are round with 3–5 shallow, blunt and toothed lobes, covered in fine down. Flowers have five mauve petals with deep purple lines converging at the centres.

DISTRIBUTION Common across Europe except the far north.

USES Young leaves and shoots have a very mild flavour and a mucilaginous texture. They may be used in salads, finely chopped in soups and stews, or as a cooked vegetable. Flowers can be used in salads. Medicinally less potent than Marsh-mallow (opposite).

Perforate St John's-wort
Hypericum perforatum

SIZE AND DESCRIPTION Rhizomatous perennial to 80cm tall, the woody-based stems with two raised ridges. Leaves are stalkless and dotted with numerous translucent glands. Flowers are yellow and bear many stamens. Also called Devil's Scourge, Klamath Weed, Penny John and Rosin Rose.

DISTRIBUTION Widespread in temperate regions.

USES Foliage has an antibacterial effect. Oil from the flowers is used for dressing wounds, sunburn, neuralgia, anxiety and depression. The herb can affect several prescription drugs, and if taking any, a qualified professional must be consulted.

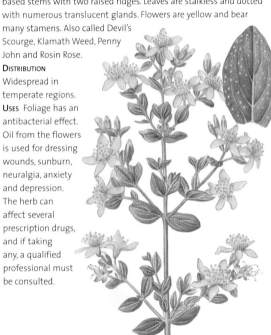

Sweet Violet
Viola odorata

SIZE AND DESCRIPTION Creeping perennial to 15cm tall, with a rosette of kidney-shaped leaves and long rooting stolons. Long-stalked flowers are spurred, and dark violet or white. Also called English Violet, March Violet and Sweet Pansy.

DISTRIBUTION Native throughout much of Europe.

USES Flowers form the base for perfume and for a wine. They can be candied and used as cake decorations, and added fresh to salads and desserts. Contains methyl salicylate, from which aspirin is derived, and is a traditional treatment for headaches. Tea made from the leaves, or a syrup made from the flowers, is used to soothe bronchial complaints and coughs.

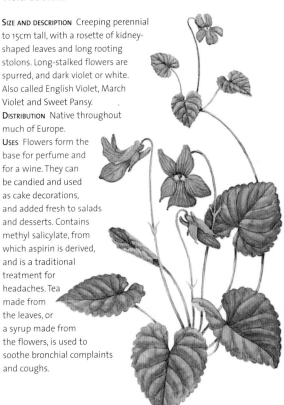

Heartsease
Viola tricolor

SIZE AND DESCRIPTION
Branching hairless or downy-
hairy annual, biennial or perennial
to 12cm tall. Lower leaves are ovate,
upper leaves oblong. Flowers are
yellow, violet or bicoloured, and
unequal; the lower petal bears a
spur 6mm long. Also called Wild
Pansy and Love Lies Bleeding.
DISTRIBUTION Most of Europe.
USES Flowers can be added to salads or used to decorate desserts.
Has been used for gout, arthritis and respiratory disorders, and in
ointment form for eczema and acne.

Tasmanian Blue Gum
Eucalyptus globus

SIZE AND DESCRIPTION Large, fast-growing
evergreen tree to 40m tall, with grey-brown
bark that peels away in strips. Juvenile leaves
are bluish, opposite and clasp the stem; adult
leaves are dark green, alternate and drooping.
Flowers are woody cups with numerous
stamens and no petals or sepals.

DISTRIBUTION Native to Australia, and
planted in many other parts of
the world.

USES Eucalyptus oil, distilled
from the adult leaves, is a
strong antiseptic. Used in
aromatherapy in inhalants
and decongestants, as a
chest rub for coughs, and
as a component of cough
sweets and pastilles.

Allspice
Pimenta dioica

SIZE AND DESCRIPTION
Evergreen tree to 9m
tall, with opposite
leathery leaves to
15cm long. Flowers
are cream and white,
and four-petalled;
male and female
flowers are carried in
clusters on separate
trees. Fruits ripen from
green to purple. Also
called Jamaica Pepper
and Pimento Bush.

DISTRIBUTION Native
to the West Indies,
and to Central and
South America;
mainly cultivated in
Jamaica, with a few
other central American counries growing it in small quantities.

USES An important ingredient in Caribbean cuisine. So named
because its flavour combines those of Cinnamon, Cloves and Nutmeg.
Green fruits are picked unripe, dried and ground. Rind is the most
aromatic part. Used in pickles, drinks, preserves and baking, and added
to many spice mixtures. Oil from the berries is used as an antiseptic.

Cloves
Syzygium aromaticum

SIZE AND DESCRIPTION
Small evergreen tree
to 15m tall, with
paired leaves.
Clustered flower
buds are at first
pale, turning green
and finally bright
red. The flowers
are seldom seen on
cultivated trees because
the unopened flower
buds, when dried, form
the cloves. Also called
Zanzibar Red Head.

DISTRIBUTION Native to
the Molucca Islands,
Indonesia, and
cultivated on Zanzibar,
and in Madagascar and
the West Indies; always
grown near the sea.

USES Cloves are used both whole and powdered to spice a variety
of culinary dishes; they are particularly associated with apples. Oil
of cloves is used in the perfume industry, as an insect repellent and
as an analgesic, particularly to counter toothache.

Common Evening-primrose
Oenothera biennis

SIZE AND DESCRIPTION Biennial with a fleshy root and leafy stems to
1.5m tall. Flowers are yellow, four-petalled, fragrant and open in the
evening. Fruits are long and slender, and contain numerous tiny seeds.
DISTRIBUTION Native to North America, and naturalized in most of Europe.
USES Root may be boiled and has a sweet flavour like parsnip. Leaves,
seeds and root are used either as an infusion or for extracting an oil.
Used for a variety of conditions, including premenstrual syndrome,
hyperactivity, high blood pressure
and arthritis, and widely employed
in cosmetics.

Witch-hazel
Hamamelis virginiana

SIZE AND DESCRIPTION Deciduous shrub or small tree to 5m tall, with smooth greyish bark. Downy-hairy leaves are widest above the middle, with scalloped margins. Flowers are yellow, appearing in clusters after the leaves have fallen; petals are strap-shaped and very narrow.

DISTRIBUTION Native to North America, and often cultivated in gardens elsewhere.

USES An astringent tannin-rich tea made from the bark or twigs was once used to treat dysentery, cholera and other ailments. Modern commercially distilled extracts and ointments are mainly used for minor bruises and scratches.

Nutmeg and Mace
Myristica fragrans

SIZE AND DESCRIPTION Evergreen tree to 40m tall, with aromatic leaves and clusters of small pale yellow flowers, the males and females on separate trees. Fruits are large and fleshy, containing a kernel, the nutmeg, enclosed in a red net, the mace.

DISTRIBUTION Native to the Molucca Islands, but cultivated in wet seaside areas elsewhere, including the East and West Indies.

USES Nutmeg and mace are dried and usually sold separately. Nutmeg is a fragrant sweet spice used grated in cooking, particularly in baking, desserts, spiced drinks, and milk- or cream-based sauces, and as a digestive tonic, though it is toxic if taken in excess. Mace is similar, but stronger and more pungent smelling; it is good with fish and in clear soups.

Chinese Ginseng
Panax ginseng

Size and description Perennial to 60cm tall, with a large root and a single whorl of palmate leaves at the top of the unbranched stem, from which emerges a long-stalked umbel of yellowish-green flowers followed by bright red fruits. Also called Korean Ginseng.
Distribution Grows in the forests of north-east China.
Uses Used in Chinese medicine for at least 5,000 years. The most highly prized of the ginsengs, regarded as a unique tonic, with the roots containing the hormone-like chemicals saponins and steroids. Reputed to counter the weakening effects of age, stress and disease, as well as to improve endurance and the ability to concentrate. Both Siberian Ginseng (*Eleutherococcus senticosus*) and American Ginseng (*Panax quinquefolius*) are closely related to the Chinese species, and are used in similar ways.

Sweet Cicely
Myrrhis odorata

Size and description Softly hairy perennial to 1.5m tall, with hollow stems and foliage smelling strongly of aniseed when crushed. Leaves are 2–3-times pinnate with oblong, lancelote, toothed and white-blotched lobes. Fruits are narrowly oblong and sharply ridged. Also called Anise, British Myrrh, Sweet Bracken and Sweet Fern.

Distribution Mountain plant from the Pyrenees, Alps, Apennines and Balkan mountains, cultivated and widely naturalized elsewhere.

Uses Sweet anise-flavoured leaves and aromatic seeds can be added to salads, whipped cream, yoghurt, light soups and dressings, or eaten on their own. Chopped leaves can be cooked with tart fruits and are a natural sweetener, safe for diabetics.

Chervil
Anthriscus cerefolium

SIZE AND DESCRIPTION Rather wiry annual to 70cm tall. Leaves are bright green, much divided and pinnate, the lobes deeply cut. Flowers are small, white and borne in umbels. Fruits are to 10mm long, including a slender beak of about 4mm.
Also called Hedge Parsley.

DISTRIBUTION Probably native to south-east Europe, and widely cultivated and naturalized elsewhere.

USES Delicate anise-flavoured leaves are used fresh in salads, vegetable, poultry, egg and fish dishes, and soups; they are best added when a dish is ready to serve to preserve the flavour. They are rich in vitamin C and minerals. Infused in tea, they may stimulate digestion and ease catarrh.

Cow Parsley
Anthriscus sylvestris

SIZE AND DESCRIPTION Biennial to 1m tall, with upright hollow stems. Leaves are 2–3-times pinnately divided. Flowers are white, and clustered in flattened umbels. Also called Wild Chervil.
DISTRIBUTION Common in northern and central Europe.
USES Young leaves have a mild aromatic taste with a hint of aniseed, and can be added to salads or used as a flavouring. Can be confused with similar-looking poisonous plants such as Hemlock.

Coriander
Coriandrum sativum

Size and description
Annual with solid ridged
stems to 70cm tall. Leaves
are 1–3-times pinnate. Fruits
are red-brown and hard, the
two halves not separating easily.

Distribution Native to North Africa
and south-west Asia, and widespread
elsewhere as both a crop and naturalized.

Uses An ancient herb known from about 1500BC. Fresh lower leaves
are used as a garnish and in curries. Ripe seeds are an ingredient of
many dishes, both sweet and savoury, and of the spice mixture garam
masala. Known as an appetite stimulant and aid to digestion.

Anise
Pimpinella anisum

Size and description
Strongly aromatic annual
to 50cm tall. Lowest leaves are
kidney-shaped, middle leaves pinnate with broad lobes, upper leaves
2–3-times pinnate with narrow lobes. Flowers are white, and are
followed by ovoid or oblong, finely ridged fruits.
Distribution Native to the eastern Mediterranean and western Asia,
and widely cultivated.
Uses Distinctively liquorice-flavoured seeds are added to dishes such
as curries, soups, cakes and pastries, and pickles. They make a relaxing
tea that may relieve tight coughs. Used in drinks such as French pastis
and Turkish raki, and in toothpastes and cosmetics.

Ground-elder
Aegopodium podagraria

SIZE AND DESCRIPTION
Stout and hairless
perennial spreading by
creeping rhizomes. Stems
are to 1m tall, hollow, and
bear leaves divided into three leaflets, each divided into three. Flowers
are white and borne in compact heads. Also called Goutweed.
DISTRIBUTION Native to Europe and Asia, and invasive in many places.
USES Young leafy shoots gathered just before flowering have a
pleasant sharp flavour, and may be used in soups and salads, or
cooked like spinach. Used traditionally for arthritis, rheumatism
and gout. An infusion or poultice can be made from the leaves.

Dill
Anethum graveolens

SIZE AND DESCRIPTION Slightly bluish, strongly smelling annual to 50cm tall, similar to Fennel (opposite), with much-divided feathery leaves and yellow flowers. Fruits are bordered with a pale wing. Also called Anet, Dill-oil Plant and Sabbath Day Posy.

DISTRIBUTION Probably native to south-west Asia, and widely cultivated and naturalized in many temperate regions.

USES An ancient culinary herb. Leaves are added to fish dishes, soups, stews and cream sauces. Stronger tasting aromatic seeds are used to spice pickles, vinegar and vegetables. Oil of dill is a mild sedative, and dill water, made by infusing bruised seeds, is said to improve the appetite and digestion, and to ease colic.

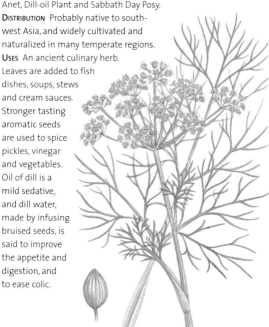

Fennel
Foeniculum vulgare

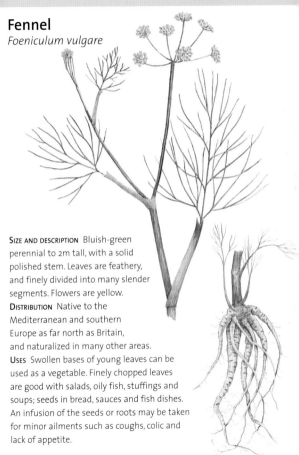

SIZE AND DESCRIPTION Bluish-green
perennial to 2m tall, with a solid
polished stem. Leaves are feathery,
and finely divided into many slender
segments. Flowers are yellow.
DISTRIBUTION Native to the
Mediterranean and southern
Europe as far north as Britain,
and naturalized in many other areas.
USES Swollen bases of young leaves can be
used as a vegetable. Finely chopped leaves
are good with salads, oily fish, stuffings and
soups; seeds in bread, sauces and fish dishes.
An infusion of the seeds or roots may be taken
for minor ailments such as coughs, colic and
lack of appetite.

Cumin
Cuminum cyminum

SIZE AND DESCRIPTION Slender annual to 50cm tall. Leaves are divided into thread-like lobes. Flowers are white or pink, and there are 3–5 in each of the simple small umbels that form the compound umbel. Fruits are to 5mm long and finely ridged.

DISTRIBUTION Native to North Africa and south-west Asia, and widely cultivated elsewhere.

USES Whole or ground seeds are used in Asian and North African cuisines, and often added to spice mixtures. Can be used in curries, and with chicken, lamb and beef dishes, soups and preserved meats. Closely related to Caraway (page 91) and similarly used for digestive complaints.

Wild Celery
Apium graveolens

SIZE AND DESCRIPTION Biennial to 1m tall. Lower
leaves are pinnate, upper leaves divided
into three leaflets. Flowers are
greenish-white, and followed
by ovoid fruits.

DISTRIBUTION Found in Europe,
Asia and North Africa.

USES Cultivated Garden
Celery (*A. g. dulce*) is less
pungent in taste and more
commonly used. Young
leaves can be added to
salads, the seeds to stews;
seeds are often used in
the form of celery salt.
Swollen blanched leaf
stalks of the garden
form are the well-
known vegetable.
Said to help arthritis,
gout, fluid retention
and fungal infections.

Garden Parsley
Petroselinum crispum

SIZE AND DESCRIPTION Stout-rooted biennial to 40cm tall, with a solid stem and sharply ascending branches. Leaves are three-times pinnate and shiny green. Flowers are yellow.

DISTRIBUTION Probably native to south-east Europe or western Asia, and cultivated and naturalized in every temperate region.

USES Curly and frilled leaves of some cultivated forms are a popular culinary garnish. They are also a breath freshener recommended against the smell of garlic, and a good source of vitamin C and iron. Said to help urinary disorders and fluid retention, and used to dress insect bites and wounds.

Caraway
Carum carvi

SIZE AND DESCRIPTION
Much-branched
biennial to 60cm tall,
with hollow and faintly
grooved stems. Leave are 2–3-
times pinnate, with segments
divided into narrow lobes. Flowers are white or pink. Fruits
are ellipsoid and ridged.

DISTRIBUTION Found in temperate regions of the Old World;
introduced in many areas.

USES An ancient herb cultivated on a large scale today. Used as a
flavouring ingredient, the seeds are also a good appetite stimulant;
they are widely used in cooking. Leaves have a flavour similar to that
of Dill (page 86) and may be used in salads; the roots can be cooked
as a vegetable. Used in proprietary medicines for digestive disorders.

Garden Angelica
Angelica archangelica

Size and description Hardy biennial to 3m tall, with stout and ridged, hollow green stems. Flowers are greenish. Fruits have broad corky wings. Also called Angel's Fishing Rod and Ground Ash.

Distribution Throughout northern Europe and Greenland to Central Asia.

Uses Best known for the candied stems of confectionery. High sugar content. Fresh leaves are added to soups, fish and stewed fruits, the seeds used as a flavouring for liqueurs such as Chartreuse and Benedictine. A tea from the seeds or dried roots is said to help anaemia, colds, asthma and other bronchial conditions. Used as a digestive tonic in herbal medicine. The herb should not be taken in larger than culinary amounts – very large doses can stimulate, then paralyse the nervous system.

Lovage
Levisticum officinale

Size and Distribution Stout and strong-smelling perennial to 2.5m tall. Leaves are 2–3-times pinnate, the lobes deeply and irregularly toothed. Flowers are greenish-yellow. Fruits are to 7mm long, ridged and winged. Also called Bladderseed.
Distribution Native to Iran, and cultivated and naturalized in other regions of the world.
Uses Strong flavour reminiscent of celery. Young leaves and seeds may be added to many dishes, including vegetarian ones, seeds to breads and other savouries. Also employed in herb liqueurs. Used for digestive complaints and to reduce water retention.

Scots Lovage
Ligusticum scoticum

SIZE AND DESCRIPTION Perennial to 80cm tall,
with thick stems. Leaves are large, 2–3-times
pinnate, with diamond-shaped lobes and toothed
margins. Flowers are yellow, and borne in dense
compound umbels. Much smaller than Lovage (page 93).
DISTRIBUTION Locally common in coastal Scotland, Northern
Ireland and northern Europe, growing near the sea and on sea cliffs.
USES Leaves have a strong celery aroma. They are good for reinforcing
the flavour of vegetable soups, and may be wrapped around red meat
joints for roasting. They were once eaten in Scotland to prevent scurvy.

Alexanders
Smyrnium olusatrum

SIZE AND DESCRIPTION Strong-smelling biennial to 1.25m tall. Leaves are dark green, shiny and divided into three, each segment with three lobes and a toothed margin. Flowers are yellow, with up to 15 simple umbels forming a compound umbel.

DISTRIBUTION Naturalized and common on the coasts of southern Britain and other parts of Europe.

USES Should be picked before the flowers open. Stems can be boiled or steamed for a few minutes; the aniseed smell disappears with cooking, and they can be eaten like asparagus. Young leaves are good in salads, or chopped into a sauce made with butter, flour and milk.

Asafoetida
Ferula assa-foetida

SIZE AND DESCRIPTION

Foul-smelling yellowish perennial to 2m tall, with stout grooved stems and thick roots. Leaves are to 35cm long, and deeply 2–4-times divided. Flowers are pale greenish-yellow and produced in large and flat compound umbels; flower spikes can reach 4m in height. Flowers are followed by fruits 1.2cm long. Roots are thick and pulpy. Also called Devil's Dung, Stinking Gum, Hing, Food of the Gods and Giant Fennel.

DISTRIBUTION Native to Iran; also cultivated in India and Afghanistan.

USES Asafoetida is a waxy gum resin derived from the root and stem of this and two similar species. As a condiment, mainly used in Persian, Afghan and Indian cuisines, especially in vegetarian dishes. Plant smells strongly due to the presence of sulphur compounds, but the smell disappears after cooking. Used for digestive complaints and lowering blood pressure, and in veterinary medicine.

Pignut
Conopodium majus

SIZE AND DESCRIPTION Almost hairless perennial to 25cm tall, with slender stems and finely divided upper leaves. Flowers are white, with 6–12 simple umbels arranged in a compound umbel. Root tuber is dark brown and irregular.

DISTRIBUTION Common in western Europe eastwards to Italy.

USES Dark brown, irregular root tuber has a taste reminiscent of hazelnuts, and can be peeled, washed and eaten raw. Powdered roots have been said to make a good cough remedy.

Wintergreen
Gaultheria procumbens

SIZE AND DESCRIPTION
Creeping evergreen
shrub to 15cm tall.
Leaves are thick,
leathery and shiny-
dark. Flowers are
white, waxy,
drooping and bell-
shaped. Berries are
globose and bright
red, and they persist
throughout winter. Also called
Boxberry, Squaw Plum and Drunkards.

DISTRIBUTION Native to northern and eastern North America.

USES Fragrant leaves contain methyl salicylate, which is similar to
aspirin and may be useful for combatting rheumatism. It is extracted
as an oil; the oil content of frosted leaves, which turn purple, is
thought to be higher than that of unfrosted leaves. The natural oil
has now been largely replaced by synthetic compounds.

Bilberry
Vaccinium myrtillus

Size and description Small, much-branched evergreen shrub with green twigs. Leaves are bright green and oval, with slightly toothed margins. Flowers are globose, with fused greenish-pink petals. Fruits are globose blue-black berries. Also called Blaeberry and Whortleberry.

Distribution Occurs throughout temperate and subarctic regions of the world.

Uses Very sweet and with a high vitamin C content, the fruits can be eaten raw and, where abundant enough, used in pies, preserves, jellies, fruit stews and wine. Reputed to improve night vision and help eye disorders such as macular degeneration.

Cranberry
Vaccinium oxycoccos

SIZE AND DESCRIPTION Small, spreading
evergreen shrub to 12cm tall, with dark
green leaves. Flowers have a pinkish-red corolla
deeply divided into four lobes. Fruits are globose
red berries. Also called Crone Berry, Fen Grapes
and Moorberries.

DISTRIBUTION Occurs in cooler parts of the northern hemisphere.

USES Fruits are very acidic and almost inedible raw, but where they
are abundant they can be used to make jams, jellies and fruit stews.
Used to help prevent cystisis and recurrent urinary infections.

Great Yellow Gentian
Gentiana lutea

SIZE AND DESCRIPTION Stout and erect perennial to 1.2m tall. Leaves are opposite, large, ribbed and clasping; those towards the stem form a rosette. Flowers are yellow with 5–9 corolla lobes. Also called Feldwode and Yellow-flowered Gentian.

DISTRIBUTION Confined to the mountains of central and southern Europe, where it grows in grassy subalpine and alpine pastures.

USES All gentians contain very bitter principles, which in this species are obtained from the dried roots. Once regarded as something of a universal panacea, the bitters may aid a variety of digestive ailments. Should not be taken in pregnancy or if suffering from high blood pressure.

Common Jasmine
Jasminum officinale

SIZE AND DESCRIPTION
Deciduous or semi-
evergreen woody
climber to 10m tall.
Leaves are opposite,
pinnate, and have 5–7
leaflets. Flowers are
usually white, but may
sometimes be flushed
purple; they are
fragrant and tubular.
Also called Jessamine,
Poet's Jasmine and
Summer Jasmine.

DISTRIBUTION Native to
south-west Asia.
Introduced to Europe
in the 16th century,
and now extensively
grown in different
areas of the world,
including as an
ornamental garden plant in Britain, where it is valued for its scent.

USES Jasmine oil is an expensive, powerful fragrance obtained from
the flowers. It has a rich, warm floral scent and is used by perfumers,
as well as by aromatherapists for depression and as a relaxant.
Jasmine tea is a mild sedative and may ease headaches. Essential oil
should not be taken internally; berries are poisonous.

Bogbean
Menyanthes trifoliata

SIZE AND DESCRIPTION Aquatic plant 12–35cm tall. Leaves are divided into groups of three leaflets and held above the water's surface. Flowers are pink and white with fringed petals, and borne in spikes. Also called Bitterwort, Bog Hop and Water Trefoil.

DISTRIBUTION Native to still water and bogs across most of the temperate northern hemisphere.

USES Used for flavouring ales and other alcoholic drinks. Traditional tonic and purging herb, the leaves and rhizome containing bitter compounds similar to those in gentians (page 101). Recommended for various complaints, stimulating the appetite, but may cause vomiting in large doses.

Woodruff
Galium odoratum

SIZE AND DESCRIPTION Slender fragrant perennial to 25cm tall, with creeping rhizomes and erect stems. Leaves usually 6–9 in each whorl, their margins with tiny, forwards-pointing teeth. Flowers are white and fragrant, forming dense clusters. Also called Hay Plant, Kiss-me-quick and Sweet Grass.

DISTRIBUTION Found in woodland throughout much of Europe, North Africa and northern Asia.

USES Leaves and flowers make a good tea and are used to flavour wines for May cups; flowers can be added to salads. A traditional strewing herb containing coumarin, the compound that gives new-mown hay its distinctive scent. It is contained in some medicines that are used for treating haemorrhoids and preventing thrombosis.

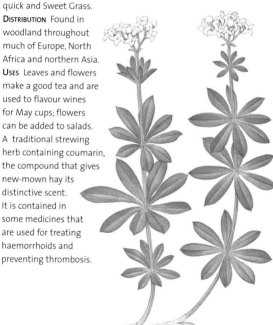

Lady's Bedstraw
Galium verum

SIZE AND DESCRIPTION Perennial to 60cm tall, with creeping stolons and much-branched and four-angled stems. Leaves are very narrow, and borne in whorls of 8–12. Flowers are bright yellow, four-lobed and form a branched spike. Also called Bed Flower, Cheese Rennet and Maid's Hair.

DISTRIBUTION Native to grassland throughout most of Europe and western Asia.

USES Once used as a stuffing for mattresses, hence its name, but most of its old uses were connected with curdling milk. It is said to be less effective with modern milk, though it can still be used to impart a rich yellow colour to cheese.

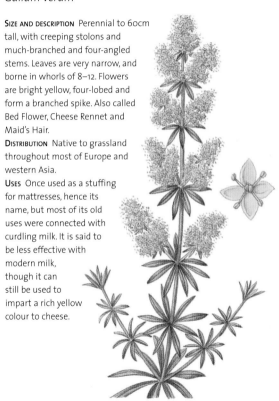

Cleavers
Galium aparine

SIZE AND DESCRIPTION Rough and minutely prickly annual that scrambles through surrounding vegetation. Stems reach 1.5m and are four-angled, with 6–9 leaves in each whorl. Flowers are tiny, whitish and four-lobed. Fruits are burr-like, and consist of two fused globes covered with hooked bristles. Also called Goose Grass, Bur Weed, Scratch Weed and Stick-a-back.

DISTRIBUTION Native across Europe, and northern and western Asia.

USES An infusion from the dried aerial parts may be used as a diuretic for cleansing the lymphatic system and reducing swollen glands. It may also help against eczema, psoriasis, sores and wounds, and dandruff.

Yellow-bark
Cinchona calisaya

SIZE AND DESCRIPTION Evergreen tree to 12m tall. Leaves are oval to oblong. Flowers are small, fragrant, pink, white or red, and borne in terminal clusters. Fruit is a small capsule containing many seeds.

DISTRIBUTION Native to the eastern Andes in South America, and introduced to Asia, where it is grown on plantations. Also called Peruvian Bark, Crown Bark and Fever Tree.

USES The flavouring used in tonic water. Bark contains a large number of alkaloids, particularly quinine, which is used for fevers and heart problems, and is the most effective treatment for malaria. It can be toxic, and as a drug should only be used under medical supervision.

Lungwort
Pulmonaria officinalis

SIZE AND DESCRIPTION Hairy perennial to 30cm tall, with clumps of white-spotted, unstalked and clasping stem leaves and spoon-shaped basal leaves. Flowers are pink and blue, funnel-shaped and carried in terminal clusters on leafy stems. Also called Bedlam Cowslip, Mary's Tears, Soldiers and Sailors, Jerusalem Sage and Spotted Dog.

DISTRIBUTION Occurs mainly in central and southern Europe, northwards to Britain and Sweden, as well as in northern parts of the United States.

USES Due to the leaves' supposed similarity to lungs, an infusion of leaves was in the past used as a remedy for pulmonary ailments. This traditional use has been confirmed, the leaves containing soothing mucilage and silica that may restore elasticity to the lungs.

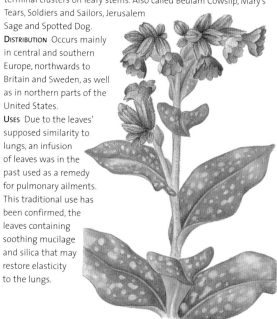

Common Comfrey
Symphytum officinale

SIZE AND DESCRIPTION Erect bristly perennial to 1.2m tall. Basal leaves are oval and hairy; stem leaves are shorter and often clasp the stem. Flowers are purple-violet, pinkish or white, tubular to bell-shaped, and carried in curved sprays. Also called Bruisewort and Bone-set.
DISTRIBUTION Occurs in most of Europe.
USES Reputed to have healing properties due to the presence of allantoin, and a poultice of the leaves or roots may be effective for bruises, ulcers and burns. Should not be taken internally. Prolonged use is reported to cause liver damage.

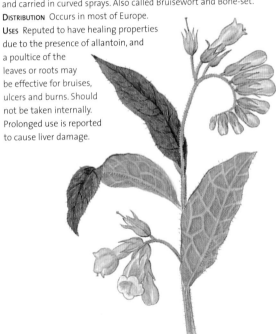

Borage
Borago officinalis

SIZE AND DESCRIPTION
Erect bristly annual
to 60cm tall. Basal
leaves are stalked;
upper leaves are
stalkless and clasp
the stem. Flowers are
blue, with five spreading,
pointed corolla lobes; black
stamens form a central cone.
Also called Cool Tankard
and Talewort.

DISTRIBUTION Native to southern Europe, and widely cultivated and
naturalized elsewhere.

USES Young leaves taste of cucumber and can be added to salads
and drinks. Flowers make a good garnish for salads, and sweet and
savoury dishes. They may also be crystallized for cake decoration.
The herb has a long history of medicinal use, including as a tea
for easing coughs and depression.

Vervain
Verbena officinalis

SIZE AND DESCRIPTION Erect
perennial to 60cm tall,
with tough and
slender, F-angled
stems. Leaves are
opposite and
pinnately lobed.
Flowers are pale
pink, slightly two-
lipped and borne on
long slender spikes. Also
called Enchanter's Plant, Herb Grace, Herb of the Cross, Juno's Tears
and Tears of Isis.

DISTRIBUTION Occurs from Europe and North Africa to the Himalayas.

USES Long tradition of magical and medicinal use. Tea made from
the aerial parts is said to help nervous exhaustion, headaches and
migraine. Also thought to be effective against liver and gall-bladder
disorders. Should not be taken during pregnancy.

Lemon Verbena
Aloysia citrodora

Size and description Deciduous shrub to 8m tall in the tropics, but much smaller in cooler regions. Leaves are narrow, yellowish-green and borne in whorls of three. Flowers are pale lavender, two-lipped and grouped in slender terminal spikes.

Distribution Native to South America, and widely cultivated in the Mediterranean and other parts of the Old World.

Uses Used sparingly, the fresh young leaves impart a lemon flavour to fruit dishes, apple jelly, stuffings and poultry. Essential oil extracted from the plant is used in perfumes and liqueurs. Aerial parts are strongly lemon-scented when crushed, and used as a tea to improve digestion. Said to counter insomnia, depression and lethargy.

Sweet Basil
Ocimum basilicum

SIZE AND DESCRIPTION Perennial or, in cool regions, an annual to 50cm tall. Opposite leaves are hairless and slightly fleshy. Flowers are white or mauve-tinged, two-lipped and borne in whorls, forming a loose spike. Many varieties, including purple-leaved forms.

DISTRIBUTION Native to tropical Asia, and cultivated in many parts of the world.

USES Fresh leaves are the main ingredient in pesto sauce and can be used in many other dishes; they are particularly complimentary to preparations based on tomatoes. Grown indoors, Basil may act as an insect repellent. One of more than 60 basil species with a variety of fragrances, including lime, lemon, cinnamon, thyme, anise and sweet camphor.

Virginian Skullcap
Scutellaria lateriflora

SIZE AND DESCRIPTION
Perennial to 1m tall.
Leaves are opposite, ovate
to lanceolate and toothed.
Flowers are blue, two-lipped
and borne in one-sided
axillary spikes; each calyx
has a distinctive shield-
shaped flap on the
upper side. Also called
Blue Pimpernel and
Mad Dog Weed.
DISTRIBUTION Native to
North America.
USES Used in small doses
to counter insomnia,
depression and other
nervous conditions (consult
a trained herbalist).

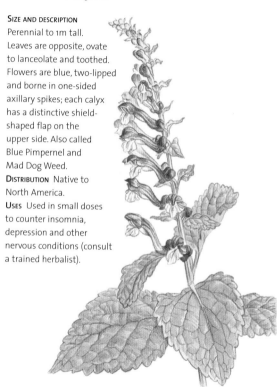

White Horehound
Marrubium vulgare

SIZE AND DESCRIPTION
White-felted
perennial to 60cm
tall. Wrinkled leaves
are opposite and
rounded. Flowers
are white with a
deeply bifid upper
lip and a calyx tube
with ten tiny hooked
teeth at the rim.

DISTRIBUTION
Native across
Europe and North
Africa, as far as
central Asia.

USES Used as a
cough remedy
since ancient
times. Has also been
used for heart, liver and
digestive problems, and
as a quinine substitute for
malaria, but now mainly
employed for respiratory conditions. Horehound candy is sold as
cough sweets. Aerial parts yield bitter principles and a volatile oil,
and can be taken as a hot or cold infusion, or as a syrup. Should
not be used during pregnancy.

Motherwort
Leonurus cardiaca

SIZE AND DESCRIPTION Strong-smelling perennial to 1.2m tall. Leaves are opposite, and cut into 3–7 toothed lobes that radiate from the leaf base. Flowers are white or pale pink with densely hairy upper lips, and carried in compact whorls. Also called Cow Wort, Lion's Mane and Lion's Tail.

DISTRIBUTION Originated in Central Asia and now found throughout the world. Introduced to Britain during the Middle Ages.

USES Used mainly for menstrual problems, and post-natal and menopausal anxiety, as well as for heart complaints. Flowering herb makes a bitter tea, and is more normally taken as a syrup or in tablet form. The herb should never be used during pregnancy.

Lemon Balm
Melissa officinalis

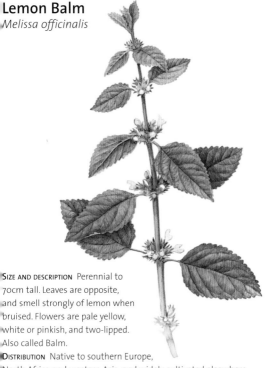

SIZE AND DESCRIPTION Perennial to
70cm tall. Leaves are opposite,
and smell strongly of lemon when
bruised. Flowers are pale yellow,
white or pinkish, and two-lipped.
Also called Balm.

DISTRIBUTION Native to southern Europe,
North Africa and western Asia, and widely cultivated elsewhere.

USES Fresh leaves are used to flavour drinks, cheeses, jellies, jams and
preserves. The herb has a long history of use as a cordial and tea,
particularly as a sedative and digestive aid, and for treating nervous
conditions and viral infections.

Betony
Stachys officinalis

SIZE AND DESCRIPTION Perennial to 50cm tall, with sparsely leafy stems and a well-developed basal rosette of long-stalked, oblong leaves. Flower whorls are crowded onto spikes; corollas are bright reddish-purple and two-lipped, the upper one flat.

DISTRIBUTION Native to Europe.

USES An ancient herb long held in high regard for its allegedly protective and curative powers, but it has fallen into disuse. Traditionally used as a poultice of fresh leaves to clean wounds; dried leaves were used to provoke violent sneezing to clear head colds. Today used mainly in herbal smoking mixtures.

Hyssop
Hyssopus officinalis

SIZE AND DESCRIPTION Aromatic perennial or miniature shrub to 60cm tall, with stems that are woody at the bases. Leaves are narrow and opposite. Loose whorls of two-lipped blue or violet flowers are carried on slender spikes at the stem tips.

DISTRIBUTION Native to southern Europe, North Africa and western Asia, and cultivated elsewhere.

USES Flowers can be used in salads. Volatile found in the herb contains the bitter principle (marrubin) that is also present in White Horehound (page 115); medicinally, the plants are used in similar ways. Should not be used during pregnancy.

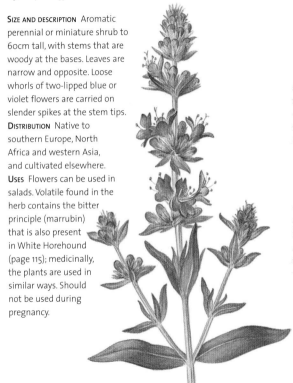

Summer Savory
Satureja hortensis

SIZE AND DESCRIPTION Annual to
25cm tall. Leaves are narrow and
opposite. Flowers are white,
pink or lilac, and carried in
few-flowered whorls. Both
the calyx and corolla are
two-lipped, the calyx with the lower teeth slightly longer than the
upper. Also called Satyricon and Stone Basil.

DISTRIBUTION Native to the Mediterranean, and widely cultivated.

USES A culinary herb with a strong, hot and peppery taste, used with
vegetable, bean and meat dishes. Said to ease the pain of bee stings
if rubbed on them, and taken in tea form as an appetite stimulant
and digestive aid.

Common Sage
Salvia officinalis

SIZE AND DESCRIPTION
Aromatic greyish shrub
to 60cm tall, with woolly
branches. Leaves are
opposite, and wrinkled
above and densely
hairy beneath. Flowers
are violet-blue, pink or
white, and two-lipped.

DISTRIBUTION Native to the eastern and western Mediterranean,
and widely cultivated in other parts of the world.

USES Improves the keeping quality of meat and processed foods,
and leaves are added to various sausages, pickles, cheeses and honey.
Medicinally, it is less used than it once was, but is still regarded as
effective for colds, and mouth and throat infections. Essential oil
is used to flavour wines and liqueurs, and in perfumed products.
Essential oil or dried herb can be used as a moth repellent.

Oregano
Origanum vulgare

SIZE AND DESCRIPTION Often purple-tinged, rather woody and aromatic perennial to 90cm tall. Leaves are opposite and stalked. Flowers are white or purplish-pink, two-lipped and carried in small spikes crowded into terminal flat-topped clusters. Also called Wild Marjoram.

DISTRIBUTION Native to the Mediterranean and Middle East, and widely cultivated in other parts of the world.

USES More pungent scent and stronger flavour than that of Sweet Marjoram (opposite), and thus more robust and can withstand longer cooking without losing its aroma. Leaves are used fresh or dried, particularly in Italian and Mediterranean cuisines, and in various meat products such as sausages. Aids the digestion and acts as an antiseptic; also used for bronchial complaints. Essential oil is used in some liqueurs, perfumes and cosmetics.

Sweet Marjoram
Origanum majorana

SIZE AND DESCRIPTION Similar to its close relative, Oregano (opposite), but generally smaller in all its parts, reaching a height of 30cm, with more or less stalkless leaves. Flowers have a one-lipped calyx that is deeply slit on one side. Also called Knot Marjoram and Pot Marjoram.

DISTRIBUTION Native to North Africa and south-west Asia, cultivated in other regions and naturalized in southern Europe.

USES Introduced to Europe in the 16th century, when it was used in nosegays to ward off the plague and other diseases. More delicately flavoured and sweetly scented than Oregano. Fresh or dried leaves are used in lightly cooked dishes with vegetables, eggs or cream. Tea may help to ease colds and aid the digestion. Essential oil is used in perfumes and cosmetics.

Common Thyme
Thymus vulgaris

SIZE AND DESCRIPTION
Miniature aromatic
shrub to 30cm tall,
with erect or spreading
branches. Leaves are
opposite, narrow and greyish-
green. Flowers are white to
pale purple, and two-lipped.

DISTRIBUTION Native to the western Mediterranean, and
cultivated elsewhere.

USES Widespread and popular culinary flavouring. Fresh or dried
leaves can be added to almost any savoury dish. Strong antiseptic
properties. Thyme oil is used in mouthwashes and cough medicines,
and in some cosmetics and toothpastes. Oil can be toxic if taken
internally, and should not be used during pregnancy.

Wild Thyme
Thymus serpyllum

SIZE AND DESCRIPTION Mat-forming perennial to 5cm tall. Leaves are opposite and small. Flowers are purple, two-lipped and grow in dense terminal clusters. Also called Creeping Thyme and Mother of Thyme.

DISTRIBUTION Common in Europe in dry grassland, heaths, dunes and screes from southern Sweden southwards.

USES Excellent aromatic herb that can be used in savoury dishes and poultry stuffings.

Spear Mint
Mentha spicata

Size and description Strongly
aromatic perennial to 90cm tall.
Leaves are narrow-ovate, toothed and almost unstalked. Flowers are
lavender, and carried in tall and slender spikes.

Distribution Earliest native origins unknown, but found across Europe
and south-west Asia. Grows in damp ground in meadows and on
verges; popular as a garden plant.

Uses The most popular cultivated culinary mint, good for mint sauce,
jelly, julep and vinegar, and with yoghurt-based dishes, potatoes and
salads. Often used in herb-tea blends.

Water Mint
Mentha aquatica

SIZE AND DESCRIPTION Strongly scented
perennial to 50cm tall, with creeping
underground stems. Leaves are greenish-
purple, opposite, toothed and oval. Small lilac flowers are densely
crowded into terminal heads to 2cm across, with additional clusters
sometimes in the axils of the upper leaves. One of at least ten other
European species of wild mint, with various flavours.

DISTRIBUTION Widely distributed in Europe's swamps, fens, marshes and
wet woods, and banks of streams, rivers and lakes; rarer in the north.

USES Slightly bitter taste, but can be used like garden mint in sauces,
chutneys, cold drinks and tea.

Pennyroyal
Mentha pulegium

SIZE AND DESCRIPTION Creeping, often mat-forming perennial to 40cm tall. Leaves are opposite, and smell like peppermint. Flowers are small, lilac and carried in dense whorls in the upper leaf axils.

DISTRIBUTION Occurs in much of Europe and North Africa.

USES Strongly flavoured leaves may be used sparsely in stews and stuffings. Hot infusion may aid coughs and asthmatic problems. Fresh leaves act as an insect repellent and alleviate bites if rubbed onto skin. Essential oil can be toxic and should never be taken without advice from a qualified medical professional.

Red Bergamot
Monarda didyma

SIZE AND DESCRIPTION Aromatic
perennial to 1.5m tall, with
square stems and opposite
leaves. Flowers are bright red,
tubular, two-lipped, 2–3cm
long and crowded together
in showy and dense
terminal clusters.
Name of the plant
derives from the
attractive scent of its
foliage, which resembles
that of the Bergamot
Orange (*Citrus bergamia*).
Also called Oswego Tea
and Bee Balm.

DISTRIBUTION Native to
North America, and
now grown in Europe,
including as a garden
ornamental.

USES Leaves make
the drink Oswego
tea, named after the Oswego Indians of North America, who were
the first to use it. Flower petals make good decorations for salads.
Leaves can be used in wine cups and lemonade, or chopped and
added sparingly to salads, stuffings and jams. Therapeautically,
leaves have been used for digestive complaints and colds, as well
as to reduce fevers.

Common Lavender
Lavandula angustifolia

SIZE AND DESCRIPTION Much-branched aromatic evergreen shrub to 1m tall. Leaves are opposite, narrow and initially white-hairy, later turning green. Flowers are lavender-blue or purplish, two-lipped and borne on dense spikes.

DISTRIBUTION Native to the Mediterranean, and cultivated in other parts of the world.

USES Sometimes used to flavour sorbets and biscuits. Leaves and flowers are used in herbal teas and tobacco. Dried flowers placed in bags keep linen fresh. Lavender oil is a first-aid remedy for bites and stings. Essential oil from the flowers is used in aromatherapy for infections and stress, as well as in perfumes and cosmetics.

Rosemary
Rosmarinus officinalis

SIZE AND DESCRIPTION Aromatic
evergreen shrub to 2m tall. Leaves
are opposite, dark green above
and white-hairy beneath, narrow
and leathery. Flowers are pale
blue, and two-lipped with two
protruding stamens. Also called
Old Man and Rose of the Sea.

DISTRIBUTION Native to the
Mediterranean region, and
cultivated elsewhere.

USES Leaves add flavour to a variety
of meats, particularly lamb, sauces,
baked fish, cordials, vinegars and oils.
Essential oil, distilled from the leaves
and flowers, is added to pain-relieving
liniments, and applied directly for
headaches and to skin as an insect
repellent. Oil should not be used
internally, and very large doses
of the leaf are toxic.

White Dead-nettle
Lamium album

SIZE AND DESCRIPTION Hairy, slightly aromatic perennial to 80cm tall, with erect stems. Leaves are opposite, oval and pointed, with toothed margins. Flowers are white with a hooded upper lip, and borne in dense whorls.

DISTRIBUTION Common in much of Europe, though rare in the south.

USES Young shoots and leaves, picked before flowering, may be eaten in salads, or mixed with other vegetables and cooked like spinach. Along with the flower buds, they can be added to soups, sauces and stews.

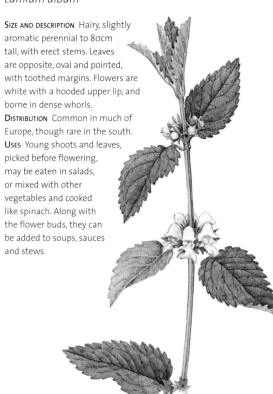

Red Dead-nettle
Lamium purpureum

SIZE AND DESCRIPTION Soft and hairy, branching annual to 30cm tall, with purple-tinged stems and a pungent scent when bruised. Leaves are opposite, heart-shaped and carried on long stalks. Flowers are pinkish-purple, and borne in whorls near the top of each upright stem.

DISTRIBUTION Common in Europe except the far north.

USES Can be used in the same way as White Dead-nettle (opposite), and the flowers may be crystallized.

Ground-ivy
Glechoma hederacea

SIZE AND DESCRIPTION Creeping perennial
to 15cm tall, with erect reddish flowering
stems. Leaves are opposite and kidney-
shaped, with shallow-toothed
margins. Flowers are pale violet,
and usually appear in pairs in
the axils of the leaf-like bracts.
DISTRIBUTION Common in Britain except
Scotland, and other parts of Europe
except the far north.
USES Once called Ale-
hoof, and employed
for making beer before
hops became popular.
Collected before flowering,
the leaves can be cooked in the
same way as spinach, and used in
vegetable soups and meat stuffings.
Dried leaves can be used to make
a tea. As a medicinal herb,
Ground-ivy is used
mainly in the
relief of catarrh
and associated
conditions
like sinusitis.

Deadly Nightshade
Atropa belladonna

SIZE AND DESCRIPTION Shrubby-looking perennial to 1.5m tall. Leaves are to 20cm long and ovate. Flowers are violet-brown to greenish, bell-shaped and drooping. Fruits are to 2cm in diameter, and glossy-black when ripe. Also called Banewort, Devil's Berries and Great Morel.

DISTRIBUTION Woodland plant native to Europe, North Africa and parts of Asia; naturalized in North America.

USES Widely used in proprietary medicines. All parts contain the narcotic alkaloid atropine, which is used as a sedative and antispasmodic for paralysing parts of the nervous system. In ophthalmology, used to dilate the pupils in eye-drops; formerly used cosmetically by women in this way (hence *belladonna*, from the Italian for beautiful woman), with prolonged use leading to blindness. The plant is highly poisonous and should never be used without medical supervision.

Sweet Pepper
Capsicum annuum

SIZE AND DESCRIPTION
Annual to 90cm tall,
with bright green leaves.
Flowers are white and
drooping, with a loose cone
of bluish-yellow stamens.
Fruits are to 27cm long,
firm and fleshy, and
ripen from green to
yellow or bright red.
There are hundreds
of varieties of Sweet
Pepper, which are
divided into groups
according to shape.
Also called Bell Pepper.

DISTRIBUTION Native to
tropical America, and
cultivated in most warm
and even temperate
regions. In areas with cool
summers, may be grown in
greenhouses and conservatories.

USES Fruits are the well-known fresh 'vegetable', and when dried
and ground the flesh of ripe red peppers yields paprika – Spain
and Hungary are the world's largest producers. Paprika is available
in many grades, from mild to hot, and can be used to flavour a
variety of dishes.

Chilli Pepper
Capsicum frutescens

SIZE AND DESCRIPTION
Tall, woody-stemmed
perennial to 2m tall.
Leaves and flowers
are similar to those
of the closely related
Sweet Pepper
(opposite), but fruits
are generally smaller,
narrower and
sometimes twisted,
and yellow, orange
or red.
DISTRIBUTION Native to
South America, and
extensively cultivated
in the tropics.
USES Chilli is used to
produce a variety of
condiments. Cayenne
powder is derived
from dried, very hot
chillies. Piri piri, the African
bird's-eye chilli, has been developed by the Portuguese into a sauce
that also includes lemons, spices and herbs. Tabasco is a well-known
hot chilli sauce invented in the United States in 1868. Medicinally,
the plant has been used externally for muscle and nerve pain, and
internally to stimulate the circulation and alleviate colds.

Thornapple
Datura stramonium

SIZE AND DESCRIPTION Annual to 2m tall. Leaves are coarse and wavy-toothed. Flowers are white to creamy or pale violet, fragrant and trumpet-shaped, and rarely open completely. Small black seeds are contained in walnut-sized, four-chambered capsules. Also called Devil's Trumpet, Loco Weed, Stinkweed and Moonflower.

DISTRIBUTION Native to North America, and naturalized in many other warm and moderate parts of the world. Grows along roadsides, in dung heaps, on wasteland and in refuse dumps.

USES Related to Deadly Nightshade (page 135) and Henbane. Contains similar alkaloids, and is likewise a narcotic. Used as a painkiller, and has been employed as an anaesthetic and for Parkinson's disease. All parts of the plant are highly poisonous and should never be eaten.

Mandrake
Mandragora officinarum

SIZE AND DESCRIPTION
Rosette-forming
perennial to 15cm
tall, with a deeply
forked taproot.
Leaves are dark
green and to 30cm
long. Flowers are
greenish-white,
sometimes with
purple staining, and
bell-shaped. Fruits are
globose, resembling
tomatoes, and ripen
from green to yellow. Also
called Devil's Apple and
Medicinal Mandrake.
DISTRIBUTION Native to
central and south-east
Europe; rare in the wild,
although cultivated in
some places.
USES With its unusual
man-shaped root, this was
one of the magical plants of ancient herbalists. A genuine medicinal
herb, the root yields a strong anaesthetic that is still used in modern
medicine. Like the related Deadly Nightshade (page 135), the plant is
poisonous and should never be eaten.

Sesame
Sesamum orientale

SIZE AND DESCRIPTION
Erect annual to 60cm
tall, with white, pink
or mauve, trumpet-
shaped flowers. Fruit
is a 3cm-long capsule
with many shiny ovoid
seeds. Also called
Halvah and Oil Plant.

DISTRIBUTION Native to
tropical Asia, and
widely cultivated and
naturalized in other hot
areas of the world.

USES First domesticated
in India in the second
millennium BC, and
grown primarily for its
oil-rich seeds. These
have a nutty flavour
when cooked and are
used as a garnish, or
ground and added to various dishes. They are often added to bread
and biscuits, and are particularly popular in eastern Mediterranean
cuisines, in which they are used to make preparations such as halva,
tahini, hummus and various sweet confections. An oil is also
expressed from the seeds. As a remedy, Sesame has been used for
dental decay, premature hair loss and osteoporosis.

Great Mullein
Verbascum thapsus

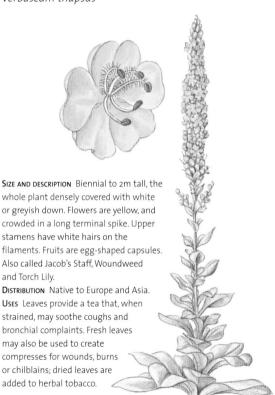

SIZE AND DESCRIPTION Biennial to 2m tall, the whole plant densely covered with white or greyish down. Flowers are yellow, and crowded in a long terminal spike. Upper stamens have white hairs on the filaments. Fruits are egg-shaped capsules. Also called Jacob's Staff, Woundweed and Torch Lily.

DISTRIBUTION Native to Europe and Asia.

USES Leaves provide a tea that, when strained, may soothe coughs and bronchial complaints. Fresh leaves may also be used to create compresses for wounds, burns or chilblains; dried leaves are added to herbal tobacco.

Common Valerian
Valeriana officinalis

SIZE AND DESCRIPTION Downy perennial to 1.5m tall, usually unbranched.
Leaves are pinnate or pinnately lobed. Flowers are pale pink, funnel-
shaped, unequally five-lobed and carried in a compound head made
up of smaller dense heads. Also
called All-heal, Herb Bennet
and Summer Heliotrope.

DISTRIBUTION Grown on damp
ground in woods and grassy
places from Europe to Japan.

USES Roots are dried
and macerated in
cold water. Used as
a sedative drug, acting on
the central nervous system,
and may help anxiety, tension
and nervous headaches. Reported
to become addictive if used for
long periods.

Eyebright
Euphrasia rostkoviana

Size and description
Erect and branched,
semi-parasitic annual to
35cm tall. Leaves are opposite
and toothed. Flowers often
have a lilac upper lip, and a white
lower lip with yellow markings. Many
closely related species.

Distribution Found in most of Europe and some adjacent areas.

Uses Aerial parts are used to make a soothing eyewash. Also used
for hayfever, colds and catarrh.

Foxglove
Digitalis purpurea

SIZE AND DESCRIPTION
Biennial or perennial
to 1.8m tall. Basal leaves
are softly hairy. Bell-
shaped flowers to 5cm
long form a long spike.
Petals are purple, pink or white,
usually spotted black inside.

DISTRIBUTION Native to western Europe.

USES Leaves yield the drug digitalin, which contains compounds
that affect the cardiac muscle to increase the heartbeat. The similar
Woolly Foxglove (*D. lanata*) from southern Europe has now largely
replaced this species in commercial production. Extremely toxic,
and can cause paralysis and sudden death if misused.

Ribwort Plantain
Plantago lanceolata

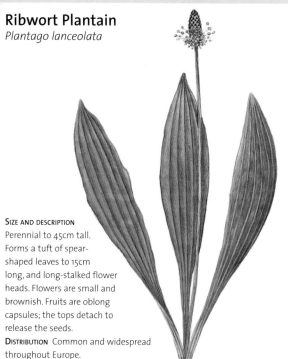

Size and description
Perennial to 45cm tall.
Forms a tuft of spear-
shaped leaves to 15cm
long, and long-stalked flower
heads. Flowers are small and
brownish. Fruits are oblong
capsules; the tops detach to
release the seeds.

Distribution Common and widespread
throughout Europe.

Uses Young leaves can be eaten in salads, but are quite bitter and
best cooked like spinach after the fibrous veins have been stripped
out. Used since ancient times as a herbal remedy. Bruised or crushed
leaves are stypic, helping to staunch bleeding and draw the pain from
bites, stings and burns. They contain mucilage, tannins and silica, and
an infusion is used for bronchitis, coughs and lung complaints.

Black Pepper
Piper nigrum

SIZE AND DESCRIPTION Perennial woody vine to 6m tall, with smooth twining stems. Leaves are alternate, large, thick and leathery. Flowers are small, greenish, petal-less and carried on long drooping spikes produced at the leaf nodes. Berries ripen from green to orange to red. Also called Madagascar Plant and White Pepper.

DISTRIBUTION Native to tropical Asia, and widely cultivated in the tropics.

USES One of the earliest and most valued of the eastern spices. With salt, a key ingredient of most savoury dishes. Black peppers are the dried unripe berries, and soaking and removing their outer skins yields the milder white peppers. Essential oil is used in rubbing oils to relieve pain and inflammation.

Elder
Sambucus nigra

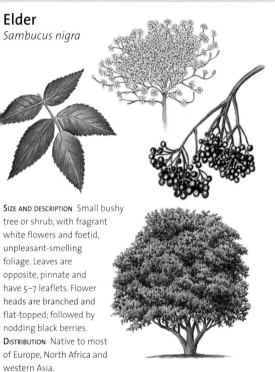

SIZE AND DESCRIPTION Small bushy tree or shrub, with fragrant white flowers and foetid, unpleasant-smelling foliage. Leaves are opposite, pinnate and have 5–7 leaflets. Flower heads are branched and flat-topped; followed by nodding black berries.

DISTRIBUTION Native to most of Europe, North Africa and western Asia.

USES Flowers and berries are traditionally used to make wines and cordials, and the berries are good in jams and pies; they should not be eaten raw. They are used as an infusion for catarrh and hayfever, as an eyewash and gargle, and to make a skin ointment. The leaves should not be eaten.

Boneset
Eupatorium perfoliatum

SIZE AND DESCRIPTION Perennial to 1.2m tall. Bases of each pair of lanceolate, wrinkled leaves are fused to encircle the stem. Flower heads consist of white or pale purple flowers carried in flat clusters.
DISTRIBUTION Native to North America.
USES Leaf tea was traditionally used by Native Americans and early settlers for fevers and influenza. Modern research suggests that it stimulates the immune system. Can be toxic in large doses.

Goldenrod
Solidago virgaurea

SIZE AND DESCRIPTION Downy perennial to 75cm tall. Leaves are lanceolate to ovate, and widest above the middle. Flower heads are yellow, with both disc and ray florets, and carried in branched spikes.

DISTRIBUTION Occurs in a variety of habitats across the northern hemisphere.

USES A mild diuretic used in many proprietary medicines for kidney and bladder disorders, catarrh, arthritis and rheumatism. May be taken as an infusion from the aerial parts collected before the flowers fully develop.

Yarrow
Achillea millefolium

SIZE AND DESCRIPTION Erect, downy and aromatic perennial to 50cm tall. Leaves are much-divided and dark green. Flower heads are carried in flat-topped clusters. Also called Milfoil.

DISTRIBUTION Native to dry grassland in Europe and western Asia, and introduced in other places.

USES A traditional herb used across the northern hemisphere. An infusion made from the dried flowering plant is used for colds and fevers. Styptic properties, helping to control internal and external bleeding, and to clear blood clots. Contains at least one toxic compound, and in large doses may cause photosensitive skin reactions.

Elecampane
Inula helenium

SIZE AND DESCRIPTION Downy
perennial to 2.5m tall. Lower
leaves are stalked, while
upper leaves are stalkless
and clasp the stem.
Flower heads have
yellow florets. Also
called Elf Dock and
Horse Elder.

DISTRIBUTION
Native to south-
east Europe and
western Asia,
and cultivated
and widely
naturalized in
other temperate
areas of the
world.

USES Used to flavour
drinks and in
confectionery. Tea
made from the
roots is employed
as a traditional

remedy for asthma, bronchitis, pneumonia and whooping cough,
and a root decoction is used to counter sciatica and skin diseases
(hence its country name, Scabwort). The plant was formerly used
to treat tuberculosis.

Sunflower
Helianthus annuus

Size and description Stout annual 3m or more tall. Flower heads may be to 30cm across, with golden ray florets surrounding the darker disc. Seeds are often striped black and white.

Distribution Native to North America, and cultivated elsewhere both commercially and as a garden ornamental.

Uses Best known as a source of high-quality edible oil, which is obtained from the seeds. Tea from the flowers is used for lung ailments and malaria; that from the leaves for fever and bites. Both can cause allergic reactions in some people.

Scented Mayweed
Matricaria recutita

SIZE AND DESCRIPTION Strongly aromatic annual to 60cm tall, with much-divided leaves. White ray florets on the flower heads are turned downwards; the yellow central disc is high-domed and hollow. Also called German Chamomile.

DISTRIBUTION Probably native to southern and eastern Europe and parts of Asia, but widespread in the wild elsewhere.

USES Tea from the dried flowers is used for colic, insomnia, hyperactivity and anxiety. Topically, used for inflamed and itchy skin conditions. May cause an allergic reaction in some people. A constituent of skin ointments and shampoos.

Wild Chamomile
Chamaemelum nobile

SIZE AND DESCRIPTION Hairy aromatic perennial to 15cm tall. Similar
to Scented Mayweed (page 153), but the flower heads have a conical
solid disc of yellow florets, and the white outer ray florets are
sometimes lacking. Also called Roman Chamomile.

DISTRIBUTION Native to
western Europe and
North Africa, and
often cultivated and
naturalized elsewhere.

USES Forms mats, and
is planted for
chamomile lawns.
Contains similar
compounds to
Scented Mayweed,
and is sometimes
used instead of
it. May cause
vomiting if taken
in excess internally.

Tansy
Tanacetum vulgare

Size and description Strongly aromatic perennial to 75cm tall, with pinnately lobed leaves. Flower heads are yellow, button-like and borne in flat-topped clusters.

Distribution Occurs in most of Europe and northern Asia.

Uses Dried aerial parts are a traditional insecticidal and vermifuge herb, once used internally and externally. Leaves can be hung indoors to deter flies, and added to insect-repellent sachets. Internal use is now discouraged because it is poisonous, the essential oil especially being fatal even in small doses.

Feverfew
Tanacetum parthenium

SIZE AND DESCRIPTION Yellowish-green aromatic perennial to 50cm tall. Leaves are pinnately lobed. Flower heads comprise dense yellow central disc florets surrounded by white ray florets. Also called Pale Maids and Pellitory.

DISTRIBUTION Native to the Balkan Peninsula and western Asia, and long cultivated and naturalized in many parts of the world.

USES A sedative tea made from the leafy parts is a traditional remedy used for arthritis, colds and cramp. More recently, the herb has received attention as a cure for migraine. Should be used with care, since it can cause an allergic reaction in some people.

Costmary
Balsamita major

Size and description Dull green, densely hairy perennial to 1.2m tall. Leaves are large, oblong and finely toothed. Flower heads are carried in branched clusters; white ray florets are sometimes absent, giving the heads a button-like appearance. Also called Alecost, Camphor Plant, Lady's Balsam and Patagonian Mint.

Distribution Native to western Asia, and widely introduced in Europe.

Uses Traditionally used to flavour beers. It has a minty or balsam-like scent. Dried leaves may be added to insect-repellent sachets. Should not be used in cooking.

Wormwood
Artemisia absinthium

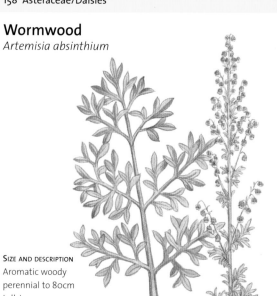

Size and description
Aromatic woody
perennial to 80cm
tall. Leaves are grey-
green, silky-hairy and 2–3
times pinnately lobed. Flower
heads contain only disc florets.

Distribution Occurs in most of Europe,
but probably introduced in some areas.

Uses One of the most bitter herbs known, and
for centuries a major ingredient in liqueurs such as absinthe. As a
herbal remedy, used as a tonic and digestive aid, and to expel worms.
It has harmful effects on the central nervous system if taken in
excess, and should not be used internally without consulting a
qualified medical professional.

Southernwood
Artemisia abrotanum

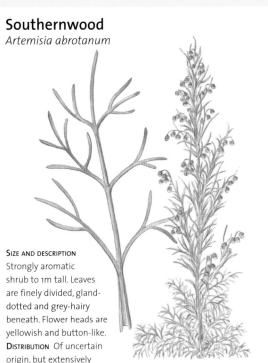

SIZE AND DESCRIPTION
Strongly aromatic
shrub to 1m tall. Leaves
are finely divided, gland-
dotted and grey-hairy
beneath. Flower heads are
yellowish and button-like.
DISTRIBUTION Of uncertain
origin, but extensively
cultivated and naturalized, especially in southern Europe.
USES Closely related to Wormwood (opposite) and similarly used as a
tonic, to expel worms and, when dried, as a moth repellent. Strongly
flavoured young leaves and shoots are bitter, with a taste of lemon
and a strong lemon scent; they are used for flavouring cakes. Should
not be used during pregnancy.

Tarragon
Artemisia dracunculus

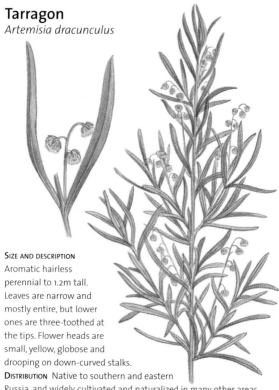

SIZE AND DESCRIPTION
Aromatic hairless
perennial to 1.2m tall.
Leaves are narrow and
mostly entire, but lower
ones are three-toothed at
the tips. Flower heads are
small, yellow, globose and
drooping on down-curved stalks.

DISTRIBUTION Native to southern and eastern
Russia, and widely cultivated and naturalized in many other areas.

USES Introduced into Britain in the mid-15th century. Used solely as
a culinary herb, in many sauces, marinades and preserves. Best used
fresh, or with the flavour preserved in oil or vinegar.

Mugwort
Artemisia vulgaris

SIZE AND DESCRIPTION Tuft-forming aromatic perennial to 1.25m tall, with reddish stems. Leaves are stalkless with pointed lobes, green and hairless above, with silky-grey hair beneath. Flower heads are reddish-yellow, growing on many short woolly spikes.

DISTRIBUTION Common throughout Europe except the far north.

USES Leaves were once used as a bitter agent in beer, and dried to make tea. Used for flavouring dripping, and in sauces and salads. In healing, it is employed as a digestive stimulant and nerve tonic.

Colt's-foot
Tussilago farfara

SIZE AND DESCRIPTION
Perennial with
flowering stems
to 15cm tall. These
appear before the large,
round, shallowly lobed
and toothed leaves,
which are green above
and white-woolly beneath.
Flowers are yellow, and borne singly on stems with purple scales.

DISTRIBUTION Occurs in damp waste places in most of the temperate
northern hemisphere.

USES A soothing tea or syrup from the leaves and flowers acts on the
mucous membranes and is used for coughs and bronchial complaints.
Dried leaves can be smoked for a similar effect and are thought to
have antihistamine properties. Potentially toxic in large doses.

Marigold
Calendula officinalis

SIZE AND DESCRIPTION Much-branched perennial to 70cm tall. Leaves are oblong to spoon-shaped, glandular-downy or sparsely woolly. Flowers are large, daisy-like, and yellow or orange.

DISTRIBUTION Possibly originated in southern Europe, and cultivated in many areas of the world.

USES Edible flowers, collected as they are opening, make excellent additions to salads and omelettes. They can be used instead of Saffron (page 180) to colour rice and cakes. They are reputed to be antiseptic, anti-fungal and antibacterial, and are employed as compresses for burns and ulcers, and for chilblains and impetigo. Calendula tincture is sometimes used as a mouthwash for gum infections and mouth ulcers.

Lesser Burdock
Arctium minus

Lesser
Burdock

Greater
Burdock

SIZE AND DESCRIPTION Coarse downy biennial to 1.5m tall. Leaves are broad, with heart-shaped bases and solid stalks. Flower heads are prickly, with only purple disc florets.

DISTRIBUTION Common throughout Europe and parts of western Asia.

USES Root is edible raw or cooked; it is best obtained from young plants, and usually peeled and sliced. Young leaves are edible raw or cooked. Young flowering stems can be peeled and eaten raw, or cooked like asparagus. Greater Burdock (*A. lappa*) is milder, and can be used in similar ways. Burdock is said to purify the blood, and is used for boils and other skin conditions.

Milk Thistle
Silybum marianum

SIZE AND DESCRIPTION Biennial to 1.5m tall. Erect
stem with stalked, spiny and white-veined
basal leaves; stem leaves are stalkless, clasp
the stem and have yellowish-white spines.
Flower heads have reddish-purple florets
enclosed by large, fleshy and spiny bracts.
DISTRIBUTION Native to southern Europe and
naturalized elsewhere. Locally common in
southern Britain; possibly native near the sea.
USES Young leaves and stems, picked before the
flowers develop and with their spines removed, can
be cooked as a vegetable. Flower-head receptacles
can be used in the same
way as globe artichokes –
the outer bracts are
particularly good.
Reputed to prevent
and repair liver
damage, and used
against toxins such
as alcohol, and for
digestive and
cholesterol problems.

Blessed Thistle
Cnicus benedictus

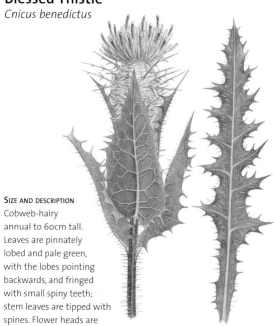

SIZE AND DESCRIPTION
Cobweb-hairy
annual to 60cm tall.
Leaves are pinnately
lobed and pale green,
with the lobes pointing
backwards, and fringed
with small spiny teeth;
stem leaves are tipped with
spines. Flower heads are
large with yellow florets, and surrounded by the upper leaves.
DISTRIBUTION Found wild in the Mediterranean, and cultivated and
naturalized elsewhere.
USES Slightly toxic in large doses, causing nausea, but a weak tea from
the flowering plant is said to be good for various ailments, from colds
to migraines, jaundice and ringworm. Mainly used as a digestive tonic
and appetite reviver.

Safflower
Carthamus tinctorius

SIZE AND DESCRIPTION
Spiny, thistle-like
annual to 60cm tall.
Basal leaves are pinnately
lobed; stem leaves are
undivided. Flower
heads have spiny,
leaf-like bracts and
numerous brilliant
yellow, orange or red
florets. Also called False Saffron and Dyer's Saffron.

DISTRIBUTION Native to western Asia, and cultivated and often
naturalized in southern and central Europe.

USES Principally a dye plant. Flowers yield red for dyeing silk, and
yellow for colouring food; sometimes used as a substitute for Saffron
(page 180). Seeds are a source of a low-cholesterol dietary oil, used
mainly as a cooking oil, in salad dressings and for making margarine.

Goat's-beard
Tragopogon pratensis

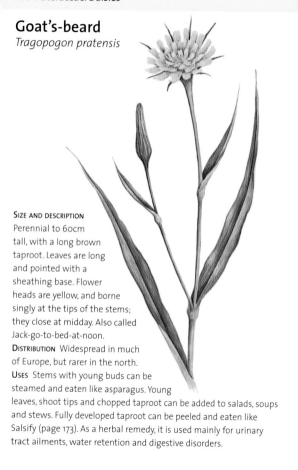

SIZE AND DESCRIPTION
Perennial to 60cm
tall, with a long brown
taproot. Leaves are long
and pointed with a
sheathing base. Flower
heads are yellow, and borne
singly at the tips of the stems;
they close at midday. Also called
Jack-go-to-bed-at-noon.
DISTRIBUTION Widespread in much
of Europe, but rarer in the north.
USES Stems with young buds can be
steamed and eaten like asparagus. Young
leaves, shoot tips and chopped taproot can be added to salads, soups
and stews. Fully developed taproot can be peeled and eaten like
Salsify (page 173). As a herbal remedy, it is used mainly for urinary
tract ailments, water retention and digestive disorders.

Cat's-ear
Hypochaeris radicata

SIZE AND DESCRIPTION
Perennial to 50cm tall, with basal
leaves only, which are long, narrow
and irregularly lobed. Flower heads consist of bright yellow florets
cupped by small scaly bracts, borne on the tips of long flower stalks.
DISTRIBUTION Common throughout Europe except the far north.
USES Young leaves can be used in salads or cooked like spinach.
Roots can be roasted and ground to form a coffee substitute.

Rough Hawkbit
Leontodon hispidus

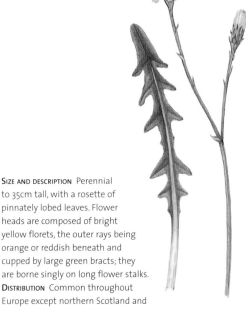

SIZE AND DESCRIPTION Perennial
to 35cm tall, with a rosette of
pinnately lobed leaves. Flower
heads are composed of bright
yellow florets, the outer rays being
orange or reddish beneath and
cupped by large green bracts; they
are borne singly on long flower stalks.
DISTRIBUTION Common throughout
Europe except northern Scotland and
the far north, growing in pastures, meadows and other grassy
places on lime-rich soils.
USES Young leaves can be used in salads or cooked like spinach in the
same way as those of Common Dandelion (opposite). An infusion of
the leaves is used for kidney complaints, dropsy and jaundice.

Common Dandelion
Taraxacum officinale

SIZE AND DESCRIPTION Perennial to 35cm tall, with a rosette of usually pinnately lobed leaves. Flower heads appear on stout hollow stalks; only yellow ray florets are present.

DISTRIBUTION Widespread in temperate grassland and on waste ground.

USES Whole plant is edible. Leaves and flowers are rich in vitamins, particularly A and C. Leaves can be used in salads or cooked like spinach. Flowers are used for wine, and buds can be pickled like capers. Dried roots can be roasted to make a coffee substitute. Leaves and fresh roots make a diuretic tea, and the herb is used as a remedy for kidney and liver ailments.

Chicory
Cichorium intybus

SIZE AND DESCRIPTION Blue-flowered
perennial with branched stems to 1m tall. Basal
leaves are pinnately lobed; stem leaves may be entire
and clasp the stem. Flower heads contain ray florets
only, and are to 3cm across and carried in small groups.
DISTRIBUTION Native to Europe, North Africa and western Asia,
and introduced to most other temperate regions.
USES Root is best known as an additive to or substitute for coffee.
Very young, blanched leaves are a popular salad vegetable. Extracts
from the roots have been used as diuretics and laxatives.

Salsify
Tragopogon porrifolius

SIZE AND DESCRIPTION
Perennial to 1.25m
tall with long linear
leaves that are wider
at the bases. Solitary
flower heads are to
5cm across, with dull
purple florets.

DISTRIBUTION Grows
in grassland, wasteland and old
cultivated ground. Native to the
Mediterranean and central Europe,
and widely naturalized through
cultivation elsewhere in Europe.

USES Dried and ground root was once used as a substitute for flour.
Flowers make attractive decorations for salads. Peeled roots can be
boiled or steamed and served on their own. When the leaves are
about 10–15cm long, they can be steamed like asparagus.

Redroot Pigweed
Amaranthus retroflexus

SIZE AND DESCRIPTION
Upright, almost
unbranched annual
to 1m tall. Leaves are
alternate, oval and pointed.
Flowers are small, and borne
in dense clusters on short spikes.
Also called Common Amaranth.
DISTRIBUTION North American species
common in southern and central Europe, including Britain, but
rarer elsewhere.
USES Young leaves have a pleasant mild flavour and may be eaten raw
in salads or cooked like spinach. When ground into flour, the seeds can
be used in soups and to reinforce the protein content of wheat flour
in breads. The plant has astringent soothing properties, and is used to
control bleeding and diarrhoea.

Aloe
Aloe vera

SIZE AND DESCRIPTION Stemless
perennial with creeping
stolons, forming
clusters of leaf
rosettes. Leaves are
to 60cm long, blue-
green and spiny,
sometimes tinged
red. Yellow flowers
are to 30mm long,
drooping and
cylindrical; carried
on spikes to 50cm
tall, they are produced
only in warm climates. Also called Barbados Aloe and Bitter Aloes.
DISTRIBUTION Native to arid areas of Africa and now cultivated in most
subtropical and tropical areas. Frequently grown as a houseplant in
temperate areas.
USES Used as a herb in the Middle East since ancient times. Often
employed in suntan lotions, hand creams, shampoos and cosmetics.
Leaves yield a soothing medicinal gel, which stimulates skin
regeneration in cuts and burns. Juice from the cut leaves is a strong
emetic and should not be used internally in fresh form.

Sand Leek
Allium scorodoprasum

SIZE AND DESCRIPTION Bulbous perennial to
1m tall, with cylindrical stems and 2–4
long and flat sheathing leaves. Flowers
are bell-shaped, pink or white, and
arranged in terminal clusters of 5–20,
enclosed by two papery sheaths. Also
called Giant Garlic, Rocambole and
Spanish Garlic.
DISTRIBUTION Locally
distributed on banks,
rough grassland and
scree edges in central
and eastern Europe,
including Britain.
USES Bulbs can be used like
garlic, and have a milder flavour.

Chives
Allium schoenoprasum

SIZE AND DESCRIPTION
Tuft-forming perennial
to 40cm tall, with narrowly
conical bulbs less than 1cm
in diameter attached to a short
rhizome. Stem and 1–2 slender
leaves are cylindrical and hollow.
Flowers are lilac to pale purple,
or rarely white, bell-shaped
and crowded in a dense umbel.
DISTRIBUTION Occurs in most of the northern hemisphere, and
widely cultivated.
USES Milder and more delicate flavour than that of the related onions,
and useful in egg dishes, salads, soups and soft cheeses. Finely
chopped leaves rather than the bulbs are used, and are best added to
dishes at the end of cooking in order for their flavour to be retained.

Wild Garlic
Allium vineale

SIZE AND DESCRIPTION Perennial to 60cm tall. Leaves are slender and hollow tubes that are grey-green in colour. Flowers are long-stalked, and are arranged in clusters protected by papery sheaths. Also called Crow Garlic.

DISTRIBUTION Native to Europe, north Africa and western Asia, growing in dry grassland and on roadside verges.

USES All parts of the plant have a strong garlic odour. Sometimes used as a substitute for garlic. Leaves can be freshly chopped into salads and dressings, and go well with seafood and lamb. Flowers may be dipped in batter and deep-fried, or added to salads. Bulbs can be used in the same way as those of cultivated garlic.

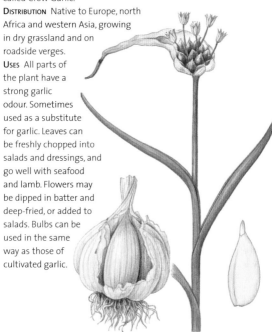

Lily-of-the-valley
Convallaria majalis

Size and description Perennial to 25cm tall. Leaves are ovate, arising from a creeping rhizome, their sheathing bases forming the stem. Bell-shaped flowers are white or pink, fragrant and carried on an erect spike. Also called May Lily, Lady's Tears and May Bells.

Distribution Native to the cool temperate northern hemisphere in Europe and north-east Asia, and a common garden plant.

Uses Leaves contain cardiac glycosides similar to those in Foxglove (page 144), and have a similar effect in regulating and strengthening the heartbeat. An essential oil from the flowers is used in perfumery and other scented products, such as soaps and hand lotions. All parts of the plant are poisonous and should only be used under medical supervision.

Saffron
Crocus sativus

SIZE AND DESCRIPTION Autumn-flowering plant with grass-like leaves that appear before the flowers. These are goblet-shaped, and lilac-purple with a yellowish throat; the prominent three-branched style is orange. Also called St Valentine's Rose.

DISTRIBUTION Does not exist in the wild. Possibly of eastern Mediterranean origin, selectively developed from *C. cartwrightianus* in ancient times.

USES Well-known food dye imparting a sweet aroma and an orange-yellow colour to rice dishes, soups and cakes. Only the large styles are used, and at least 60,000 flowers are needed to yield a pound of Saffron. As a result, it has always been expensive, and today inferior substitutes such as Turmeric (page 185) are often used instead.

Lemon Grass
Cymbopogon citratus

SIZE AND DESCRIPTION Clump-forming aromatic perennial with flowering stems to 2m tall. Leaves are to 60cm long, and tapered at both ends. Flowers are carried in a large plume-like panicle with a drooping tip. Also called Serai and Squinant.

DISTRIBUTION Native to southern India and Sri Lanka, and widely cultivated in the tropics and occasionally elsewhere.

USES Strongly scented leaves are popular in culinary use for imparting a lemon flavour to dishes. Tea made from the fresh leaves is reputed to help the digestion and elevate mood. Scent is due to the presence of citral, and oil distilled from the plant is used in the perfume industry and in the artificial synthesis of vitamin A. Also used as an insect repellent.

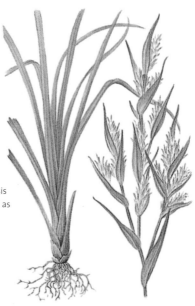

Couch Grass
Elytrigia repens

SIZE AND DESCRIPTION Dull-
to bluish-green perennial
with tough, far-
creeping rhizomes.
Flowering spikes are
to 2m long, slender,
unbranched and
composed of paired
spikelets arranged
alternately. Fruits are
small dry nutlets. Also
called Twitch, Dog
Grass, Quackgrass
and Witchgrass.
DISTRIBUTION Common
and widespread in
maritime grassland
in many regions
of the northern
hemisphere, becoming
invasive in some places.
USES Used in herbal
medicine since Classical
Greek times. Pale rhizomes are made into a tea or decoction. A
diuretic rich in minerals and vitamins A and B, the herb has antibiotic
properties and is used for kidney stones and other urinary tract
complaints.

Sweet-flag
Acorus calamus

SIZE AND DESCRIPTION
Perennial to 1m tall.
Leaves are linear, with
wavy margins, and
aromatic when
crushed. Flowers are
yellowish-green,
tiny and packed
into a compact
up-curved spike.
DISTRIBUTION Native
to southern and
eastern Asia, and
naturalized in Europe.
USES Used since
ancient times. Sweet-
scented roots are used
in herbal medicine and
perfumery. May reduce
stomach acidity and
benefit the digestion.
Also used as an
expectorant, and to
ease various respiratory
ailments. Some strains contain a carcinogen, absent from other
strains, and the herb should not be used without consulting a
qualified medical practitioner.

Ginger
Zingiber officinale

SIZE AND DESCRIPTION
Perennial to 1m tall, with short, fleshy and knobbly, branched rhizomes. Stems are erect with two ranks of leaves, the sheathing leaf stalks forming the stem itself. Flowers are yellow or white, with a purple lower lip, forming dense, cone-like spikes. Also called East Indian Ginger and Stem Ginger.

DISTRIBUTION Native to tropical South-east Asia, and also cultivated in Africa and the Caribbean.

USES Fresh or dried rhizome of Ginger, either peeled or not, is a culinary spice that is a key ingredient of Asian, African and Caribbean cuisines. The crystallized and candied stem is an ingredient in baking, jams and confectionery. Dried Ginger is used in many recipes for cakes, pastries and biscuits, as well as in commercial spice mixtures. Makes a warming and mildly stimulating remedy for the digestion, circulation and bronchial complaints.

Turmeric
Curcuma domestica

SIZE AND DESCRIPTION
Perennial to 1m tall
similar to Ginger
(opposite), to which
it is closely related,
but the leaves are
all basal, and their
sheathing stalks rarely
form a stem. Rhizomes
are about 2.5cm in
diameter, yellowish
on the outside and
deep orange within.
DISTRIBUTION Probably
native to India, and
cultivated there and
in other tropical areas.
USES Boiled, dried and
powdered rhizome
has a characteristic
pungent smell.
Widely employed as a
flavouring and colouring agent for imparting a brilliant yellow hue to
various dishes, often as a less expensive substitute for Saffron (page
180); an essential ingredient in Indian cuisine. Used in curry powders,
chutneys and pickles, and in the Moroccan spice blend *chermoula*.
Sometimes used as an antiseptic for minor cuts and burns.

Cardamom
Elettaria cardamomum

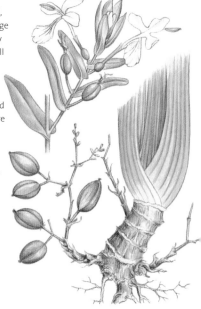

SIZE AND DESCRIPTION
Perennial to 3.5m tall, related to Ginger (page 184), with thick fleshy rhizomes and very tall sterile stems formed by the sheathing leaf stalks. Flowering stems are leafless and spreading. Flowers are white with blue and yellow markings, and a single protruding stamen. Capsules are to 2cm long, ovoid and greenish-grey, each containing 3–4 brown seeds.

DISTRIBUTION
Native to the hills of southern India, and also cultivated in Sri Lanka and parts of Central America.

USES
Capsules are harvested unripe and dried whole. Dried ground seeds are used to flavour sweet and savoury dishes, particularly in Indian and South-east Asian cuisines, and for spicing wines. Seeds have pain-relieving, antispasmodic and anti-inflammatory properties, useful for stomach disorders and urine retention.

Vanilla
Vanilla planifolia

SIZE AND DESCRIPTION
Evergreen climbing
orchid to 30m tall,
with fleshy leaves.
Flowers are to 70mm
long, and greenish-
yellow with an
inrolled, orange-
striped lower lip. Pods
are to 20cm long and
fragrant when ripe;
they contain many
tiny seeds.

DISTRIBUTION Native
to Central America,
and cultivated
throughout the
tropics, particularly
in Madagascar.

USES First used by the
Aztecs to flavour
chocolate drinks, and
introduced to Europe
by the Spanish. Unique
flavour is due to vanillin crystals on the surfaces of the pods. The pods
are used as a culinary flavouring, particularly in cakes, pastries and
desserts, though synthetic essences are also available. Commercially
used in soft drinks and liqueurs such as Galliano, and in perfumery
and fragrant household products like candles.

Arrowhead
Sagittaria sagittifolia

SIZE AND DESCRIPTION
Upright and hairless
aquatic perennial to
90cm tall, with large
tubers. Aerial leaves are
shaped like arrowheads
and borne on long
upright stalks;
floating leaves are
pointed or oval, and
lack the basal lobes
of the aerial leaves.
Flowers are about 2.5cm
wide and have three white petals, each with a purple spot at the
base. Also called Swamp Potato and Water Archer.

DISTRIBUTION Common in southern Britain and on the Continent,
except the far north and south.

USES Starchy tubers can be boiled; skins have a slightly bitter potato
flavour and they should be removed after cooking. Dried tubers can
be ground into a flour, and combined with cereal flour to make cakes
and biscuits. Tubers should not be eaten raw.

Bulrush
Typha latifolia

SIZE AND DESCRIPTION Stout perennial to 2.5m tall, with
a long, branched rhizome. Stems are erect and robust,
with long linear leaves arising from a sheathed base.
Flowers are numerous and tiny, crowded into a dense
elongated cluster. Fruits are small, dry, cylindrical and
stalked. Also called Asparagus of the
Cossacks, Marsh Pestle and Great Reedmace.
DISTRIBUTION Common at the edges of
water bodies in much of Europe;
rare in the far north.
USES The rhizome, best
collected in winter, can
be eaten raw or cooked
like potatoes, chopped
and boiled for a syrup, or
dried and ground for
thickening stews and
soups. Young vegetative
shoots may be steamed like
asparagus or stir-fried,
immature flower shoots
boiled or grilled with butter.
Said to be astringent and
anticoagulant; uses include
dressings for minor
cuts and burns.

Index

Common Names

192 Index